Fast Breads!
by Howard Early and Glenda Morris

Edited by Andrea Chesman

 The Crossing Press, Trumansburg, N.Y. 14886

The Crossing Press Specialty Cookbook Series

Early, Howard.
    Fast breads.

    (The Crossing Press specialty cookbook series)
    Includes index.
    I. Bread.   I. Morris, Glenda.   II. Title.
III. Series.
TX769 .E2   1986   641.8'15   86-19643
ISBN 0-89594-206-2
ISBN 0-89594-205-4 (pbk.)

This book is dedicated to our students, who helped us learn during our seven years of teaching bread baking at The Baltimore School. More than that, the book is dedicated to the idea that bread baking is fun.

Contents

1
Quick Notes on Quick Breads

This is a book about making quick breads. Quick breads do not require a period of kneading or rising. Generally they go straight from the mixing bowl to the oven in a bread pan, muffin tin, or tin can. Quick breads are quick. As you become comfortable with your baking, you will have your quick bread oven-ready in ten to fifteen minutes—even less if you do a bit of advance preparation.

The range of quick breads seems only as limited as the imagination. You can bake all of the basics—white, rye, whole wheat. You can select breads that are coarse and grainy, our Sunflower Rye for example, or breads that are almost like cake, such as our White Poppy Seed Bread. You can bake a quick bread with almost any fruit or vegetable, and you can bake with nuts and seeds. You can make quick breads in the style of many different cuisines—Finnish flat breads or Indian chappatis. Although we present many dessert and festive breads, most of our breads are dinner breads. Be-

cause of the variety, you can always find something that will blend uniquely with your meal.

Techniques

In most of the recipes that follow, we prepare the wet and the dry ingredients in separate containers. The dry ingredients are most conveniently assembled in a large mixing bowl. The wet ingredients can go into a one-quart jar or small bowl. Putting the liquids in a covered jar enables you to mix them by vigorously shaking the jar.

The chemistry of quick breads is such that no reaction occurs until the dry ingredients are moistened. So if you have time the night before or early in the morning, mix up the separate sets of ingredients. Then, when you are ready to bake, all you have to do is pour the wet ingredients into the bowl of dry ingredients, stir gently, spoon the batter into a well-greased bread pan, and bake.

There are a few breads in which you cut.

the butter into the dry ingredients. Those breads can't sit very long and should be baked soon after mixing.

When mixing the batter, stir quickly, but gently. Do not try to make the batter smooth; it should be coarse, but it shouldn't have big lumps. You also want to get the batter into the oven as quickly as you can (exceptions are noted). The reason for this is that as soon as you moisten the baking powder or soda, it begins to release carbon dioxide. You want that gas to be trapped in the batter to allow the bread to rise. Stir too long and too hard and much of the carbon dioxide will escape, leaving a flat, tough bread.

Bread Pans

Throughout the book we talk of small, medium-size, and large loaf pans. Large bread pans generally measure 9 inches by 5 inches. The medium-size pans are ½ to 1 inch smaller, usually 8½ inches by 4 inches. Though that may seem like a small difference, the medium-size pan holds half a pound less of batter. Small pans hold about half as much as a large pan. They generally measure 7½ inches by 3 inches.

You can, of course, bake in containers other than the traditional bread pans — any size or shape of can will do fine. Just make certain that you remove any labels and grease it well with butter or cooking oil. The best way to grease a pan is by spreading the oil with your fingers or, for the timid, by using a paper towel or pastry brush. One to two tablespoons of butter or oil is all that you need.

Flour

Any flour you find in the supermarket is fine for making quick breads. We bake with unbleached white flour. You can use all-purpose white flour just as well.

With the recent interest in using less processed foods, more people are tempted to substitute whole grains for white flour in their favorite recipes. If you do this, keep in mind three things. In a fruit bread or subtly spiced bread, the whole wheat flavor may overpower your featured ingredients. Secondly, some adjustment in the recipe may be called for because the whole wheat flour will absorb more liquid than white flour. Use slightly less flour—about one quarter to one half cup less flour for most of the recipes in this book should be about right. Finally, a bread made entirely with whole wheat flour will be much denser. You will usually get a smaller, heavier, chewier loaf. For that reason we often combine unbleached and whole wheat flours.

In selecting the type of whole wheat flour, we find that soft wheat, usually identified as pastry flour, works better than the winter or hard wheat flour used in making yeast breads. Once again, it is the amount of gluten in the flour that makes the difference. In yeast breads, developing the gluten is important to get the proper texture; in quick breads developing gluten makes the bread tough and the grain uneven.

Whole wheat flour should be stored in a cool place and kept less than three months. Because this flour contains all of the kernel (including the wheat germ), it tends to become rancid more quickly than white flour.

Your best bet for buying most flours is at a food co-op or a natural food or "health" food store. There you will be able to find all of the uncommon flours we use. Most of the stores have these flours in bulk, and that's a good deal. Bulk flour is less expensive and often fresher than packaged flour. Further, you can buy just the amount you want. So when you come to recipes that call for soy, oat, triticale, or brown rice flour, you should look for a natural food store.

Rising Agents

Baking powder and baking soda are the main leavening agents in quick breads. They both cause the bread to rise; however, they work slightly differently. All rising agents produce bubbles of carbon dioxide. The oven heat makes the bubbles expand rapidly so the dough rises. As the temperature of the dough increases to the temperature of the oven, the protein in the flour (and the milk and eggs) becomes rigid. The protein forms a solid cellular structure around the gas bubbles, creating the tiny holes that make the bread light.

Baking powder is usually a combination of one part baking soda (an alkali) and two parts of some finely powdered acid (calcium acid phosphate is among the more common). Usually cornstarch or rice flour is added to keep the mixture dry and to slow its reaction to the liquid. The baking powder will begin its rising action slowly when moistened, but its main rising action occurs when heated. This is why most of the powders on the market today are labeled "double-acting."

In breads where the liquid ingredients are highly acid, for example, buttermilk, sour cream, or orange juice, you can use just baking soda for leavening. Since the chemical interaction in these breads may be slower, the batters can be gently kneaded (as in Irish Soda Bread or some scones). Kneading helps develop the protein network that will trap the escaping gas. Since you cannot control the acid level of the liquids you use, breads relying solely on baking soda may be more variable. Sometimes, baking soda used with too little acid produces a bitter taste and brown spots in the bread itself.

Cream of tartar (tartaric acid) has been used frequently as a leavening agent. At one time it was the most common acid component of baking powder. It dissolves readily and generates gas rapidly, and so we generally use it either for stove-top breads or in combination with other rising agents. The taste of cream of tartar is inconspicuous, as is that of the other leavening agents; if you can taste them, you are using too much.

If you are starting to bake using an old

can of baking powder, you should test it beforehand. A test is simple: just add one half teaspoon of baking powder to one quarter cup of water. If it fizzes, it is still good.

A final note on rising agents. When we first began baking quick breads, we had a number of people say they couldn't eat quick breads. It "upset their stomachs," they told us. After some exploration we found the cause. Some commercial baking powders use aluminum compounds for their acid base, and a surprising number of people are sensitive to this. (This is why it is not good to cook in aluminum pans.) Do read the list of ingredients on the can and avoid those containing aluminum.

Cooking Oil, Shortening, Butter, and Margarine

You can bake with vegetable oils (corn, soybean, sunflower, and so on), with semi-solid shortenings (butter, margarine, lard), or partially hydrogenated vegetable fats (such as Crisco®). You can't bake without some sort of oil or fat and get good breads. (There are, as one might expect, a few exceptions to this rule.) The cooking oil or fat will do four things for the bread: increase the volume, soften the texture, add to the flavor, and help in maintaining freshness.

The various fats do work differently. An animal shortening, such as butter, contributes greatly to flavor and texture. A plant oil, such as sunflower oil, is tasteless, but it does make for a soft bread and coarse crumb.

Don't worry about what you use. Use what you have on hand or find convenient or economical, without falling into a rigid pattern. Vary the oils when you can and you will find that you like some better than others. For example, we find that Irish Soda Bread is particularly delicious with butter and, because of the way it is made, it does demand a semi-solid shortening.

A word about "cutting in the butter." If that is what the recipe calls for, do it. Use ice cold butter. Cut it into small chunks, say about the size of a half teaspoon or smaller, and add the chunks directly to the flour. Then using two knives, or a fork, or your fingertips, break up the chunks so that they are fully incorporated into the flour. You could also use a food processor, pulsing carefully. The flour will then look like cornmeal—it will appear grainy and yellow. Why bother? Well, what happens is that the butter melts during the baking process, creating a light, flaky texture. Make the same recipe with a liquid oil and the bread will be much denser.

Milk

Using milk instead of plain water yields a darker crust and helps the bread remain fresh longer. Like many bakers, we prefer to use nonfat dry milk as it is not always possible to have enough fresh milk on hand. If you decide to substitute dry milk for fresh milk, follow the directions on the package to get the correct proportions.

Using skim milk reduces the fat content of the bread and the calories. Incidently, since many of us do not always have fresh buttermilk on hand, powdered buttermilk is a convenient alternative.

Sweetening Agents

There are an exceptional number of sweeteners you can use in your breads. As you will see in our recipes, we often call for something other than granulated white sugar. We have tried to keep the sweeteners to a minimum for each type of bread.

Some sweeteners are fairly strong and distinctive. Molasses is a good example. Some sweeteners seem to blend better with some flours. Honey and whole wheat or maple sugar and oat are examples of fine blends. We found that in rye, triticale, and some oat breads, malted barley syrup is an excellent sweetener. It can be used in the same amounts as white sugar and it imparts a gentle taste, despite its dark color. Of course, it does add to the color of the batter. For example, it will give your white bread a light golden color. Nutritionally, it has no fewer calories, but since the glucose has already been broken down, it is easier to digest. Look for malted barley syrup in natural food stores.

There is not much difference in the nutritional value, calorie count, or the sweetness of say, one tablespoon of honey and one tablespoon of granulated sugar, or molasses, or malted barley syrup, or brown sugar. But they all have their own subtle flavor. So when you do substitute or experiment, keep those flavor differences in mind. In these recipes, substitute one sweetener for another using the same measures.

Baking Times

The baking times we give are as accurate as we can make them. However, there are so many factors that influence baking times — including the accuracy of the thermostat in your oven, the humidity, and altitude — that our time estimates may have to be reduced by as much as ten minutes. If you have doubts, check the bread every five minutes or so when it is close to getting done. When you have gained experience, you may decide that you like a particular bread drier (more time) or moister (less time), and you will set the times to suit yourself.

Try to remember how a bread felt and sounded when you removed it from the oven, and what it looked like. By the third or fourth loaf, you should begin to notice things that no amount of words can tell you.

All of these receipes have been established without preheating the oven. Most stoves move up to their temperature pretty quickly. Besides an oven that is initially too high may cause the bread to set before it has fully risen.

A few words about temperatures: If you are having difficulty with our temperatures and baking times, check your oven with a good thermometer. We have seen home ovens vary by 150 degrees. Some of the new gas ovens drop as much as 20 degrees before they fire up again.

When is the bread done? Look at the bread, thump it, poke it, listen to it, and smell it. When your kitchen fills with the wonderful smell of baking bread, you know it is getting close to being done. When it fills with smoke, you have gone too far. When the bread is still doughy, it is underdone; when it is golden brown, it is done. If you poke it and your finger sinks in, let it cook longer. If you thump it and it sounds hollow, it is done. Take it out of the oven and listen—can you hear the sound of cracking? Put it back in until the bread quiets. A totally silent loaf of bread, however, is a very well-done loaf. What you hear is the moisture evaporating.

Removing the Bread From the Pan

Some breads can be served right out of the oven, but others, especially those that are heavy in fruit or crumbly in texture, should cool first. Place the bread pan on a rack where air can circulate around all sides. Give the bread almost ten minutes to cool and contract. It should then come out of the pan quite easily. Leaving it in the pan longer can be a disaster; the crust becomes soggy from the condensation in the pan.

What if the bread sticks? First, remain calm. Be gentle with it. Run a serrated knife blade along all of the edges. If you have a wide-bladed, serrated cake knife or a spatula with a good edge, that's even better. If after loosening the sides the bread still sticks, then you will have to use your blade or spatula as a lever. Do this by leveraging it lightly along all sides. Keep working at it. You may lose a chunk, but we haven't lost a bread yet.

Eat and Enjoy

Lest you become overwhelmed by all of our bits of advice, remember that bread baking is enjoyable. You have to do something gross, such as adding a half cup of baking soda (as Glenda's brother once did) to have a total failure. While there are a few people who were weaned on supermarket white bread and cannot eat anything else, most people are genuinely excited by home-baked bread. At potluck dinners, the home-baked bread usually disappears first.

As a beginning bread baker, you might consider inviting a friend to join you in some of your first ventures. It is a great way to socialize, and we have found that two cooks don't spoil the bread.

2

Variations on White Breads and Whole Grain Breads

Quick white breads are meant to be eaten warm, as are most plain quick breads. They generally offer a lightness in body and texture that you expect to find only in more complex yeast breads. We selected our four white breads from our numerous experiments because they display a wide range of variations in taste and texture. They are a good starting point for your own variations.

The white breads here are all dinner breads and are best served with softened butter. They go well with almost any salad or main dish.

The nutritional content of different flours has been debated for at least a century. Whole wheat flour has been championed because when flour is milled and bleached into white flour some twenty nutrients are sharply reduced. The outer husk of the wheat is removed as well as the wheat germ. Both of these are valuable sources of vitamins and minerals. Just the same, we think the main reason for eating

whole wheat flour breads is because you like the taste and the texture.

Baking with oat flour will give you a delicious, different tasting bread. Because oats are low in gluten, the texture is very crumbly; however, oat breads toast well and keep well.

Oat flour is available in most health food stores. You can substitute quick-cooking oats for the oat flour; but if you do that, use about one quarter cup more unground oats. Another solution is to grind your own oats to make flour. Use any raw oats and pulverize it in your blender or food processor.

Like whole wheat, rye flour tends to produce small, dense loaves that require longer baking. Also like other whole grains, rye comes in various forms. If you find that you do not like one rye flour, say a dark rye flour, try another kind. Check out the various stores in your area and experiment with the different grinds of flour that they carry.

Rye breads are almost always enhanced by the addition of caraway seeds. We generally use a tablespoon for each loaf, although this may be too much for you.

Rye breads are ideal to serve with soups and stews. They make good solid sandwich breads, tough enough for moist fillings. Rye also goes well with sharp cheeses.

Baking with bran and buckwheat produces distinctive, strong tasting breads. Bran is the outer covering of the wheat kernel. It is coarse in texture and has a distinctive nutty taste. Bran is nutritious, but many of the nutrients are not easily absorbed. Its main contribution to diet is adding bulk, which aids the intestines in elimination. For this reason it has been highly touted in recent years as a preventative against diseases of the colon. Don't let the health benefits scare you. Bran makes wonderful, hearty breads that even our anti-whole-wheat friends like.

Buckwheat is not a type of wheat, rather it is an herb cultivated for its seeds. Because buckwheat is so pungent, we prefer to bake with light buckwheat flour. The light flour is milled from the hulled seed, while the dark flour contains the hulls. Groats are also processed from the hulled seed, but the seed is crushed into small fragments instead of being milled.

Although bran and buckwheat breads are easy to mix and handle, you should count on a baking time of about 1 hour.

Basic Semi-Sweet White Bread

Dry Ingredients

2 cups unbleached flour
½ cup sugar
2 teaspoons baking powder
½ teaspoon salt

Wet Ingredients

1 cup milk
1 egg, beaten
2 tablespoons oil

This is as simple as a quick bread can be. It is rich and cakelike, but not too sweet.

Mix together the dry ingredients.

Stir together the wet ingredients.

Combine the wet and dry ingredients very lightly. The batter will be very runny.

Pour into a greased medium-size loaf pan and bake at 350° F. for 40 minutes. Let the bread cool for 10 minutes before removing it from the pan. Cut into thick slices while still warm and serve with sweet butter.

Caraway White Bread

Dry Ingredients

1½ cups unbleached flour
1 tablespoon sugar
1 tablespoon caraway seeds
¼ teaspoon salt
2 teaspoons baking powder

Wet Ingredients

⅓ cup chilled butter
1 egg, beaten
½ cup milk

The texture of this bread is rough, and the high density of caraway seeds gives it a unique flavor and chewy texture. Caraway seeds are an aid to digestion.

Combine the dry ingredients.

Cut the butter into the dry ingredients with a pastry cutter or work it in with your fingers until the mixture resembles a coarse meal. Mix together the egg and milk.

Lightly mix together the wet and dry ingredients.

Spread the batter into a greased flat pan. An 11½-inch by 5½-inch casserole dish is ideal.

Bake at 350° F. for 30 minutes. Serve warm, directly from the pan.

This makes an easily sliced, attractive flat loaf that's about 2 inches high.

Irish Soda Bread

Dry Ingredients

2 cups unbleached flour
¾ teaspoon baking soda
½ teaspoon baking powder
1 tablespoon sugar
¼ teaspoon salt

Wet Ingredients

6 tablespoons chilled butter
½ cup buttermilk or more as needed

No quick bread repertoire would be complete without this modest light bread. As with all popular basic breads, there are many variations. Here's our version.

Mix together the dry ingredients.

Cut the butter into the dry ingredients with a pastry cutter or work it in with your fingers until the mixture resembles a coarse meal.

Pour in the buttermilk and mix gently. The batter should be moist. If it is too dry, add up to 3 more tablespoons buttermilk. The dough should be firm, not crumbly.

Knead the dough briefly and gently on a lightly floured board. (Remember this is not a yeast bread.) Shape into a round loaf.

Brush the top of the loaf with butter-

milk, and cut a cross on the top. This keeps the bread from developing random cracks on the surface; it is also the traditional pattern for Irish soda bread.

Bake on a greased baking sheet at 375° F. for 40 to 45 minutes, until it is a golden brown. Serve directly from the oven. For a more uniform appearance, you can bake it in a greased medium-size cake pan or skillet.

Variations

Some bakers add ½ cup raisins or ¼ cup currants, and sometimes a pinch of cardamom, with the buttermilk.

Garlic White Bread

Dry Ingredients

3 cups unbleached flour
1 tablespoon baking powder
½ teaspoon salt

Wet Ingredients

1 egg, beaten
¾ cup milk

Filling Ingredients

6 tablespoons softened butter
3 or more garlic cloves, crushed
2 teaspoons chopped parsley (dried or
   fresh)
⅛ teaspoon white pepper
¼ teaspoon paprika

This is a delightfully pungent bread, and you can vary the filling according to your taste and sense of adventure. Eat it warm.

Mix together the dry ingredients.

Mix together the wet ingredients.

Mix the wet and dry ingredients together. Turn the dough onto a floured surface. Knead gently a few times. Roll it out (or flatten with your hands) to a rectangle that is about 10 inches by 12 inches.

Mix together the filling ingredients. Sprinkle the filling over the dough. Roll up tightly as you would a jelly roll. Tuck the ends under and place in a large greased bread pan.

Bake at 350° F. for about 45 minutes.

Let the bread cool for 10 minutes before removing it from the pan.

Basic Whole Wheat Bread

Dry Ingredients

2 cups whole wheat flour
¾ teaspoon baking soda
½ teaspoon baking powder
½ teaspoon salt

Wet Ingredients

6 tablespoons chilled butter
1 cup buttermilk
1 tablespoon honey

This bread is our straightforward adaptation of the traditional Irish soda bread.

Combine the dry ingredients.

Cut the butter into the dry ingredients with a pastry cutter or work it in with your fingers until the mixture resembles coarse meal.

Mix together the buttermilk and honey. Mix into the dry ingredients.

Knead the dough briefly and gently.

Place in a greased medium-size bread pan or shape into a round loaf and place in a greased pie tin. Bake at 350° F. for 40 to 50 minutes.

Let the bread cool for 10 minutes before removing it from the pan.

Wheat and Soy Bread

Dry Ingredients

2 cups whole wheat flour
½ cup soy flour
2 teaspoons baking powder
½ teaspoon cinnamon
¼ teaspoon salt

Wet Ingredients

¾ cup milk
2 eggs, beaten
¼ cup oil
¼ cup molasses
½ cup raisins
Grated rind of 1 orange

Soy flour is milled from soybeans. Rich in protein, soy flour combined with whole wheat gives a high-quality protein bread. Soy flour is also rich in minerals and B vitamins so this bread is supernutritious. The soy adds a full-bodied taste to the bread.

Mix together the dry ingredients.

Stir together the milk, eggs, oil, and molasses. Add the raisins and orange rind.

Combine the dry and wet ingredients lightly.

Spoon into a small greased loaf pan or spoon into miniature greased loaf pans to make an unusual dinner roll. Bake at 375° F. for 40 minutes. For the minature loaves, reduce the baking time to 25 minutes.

Let the bread cool for 10 minutes before removing it from the pan.

Wheat-Bran-Soy Bread

Dry Ingredients

2 cups whole wheat flour
½ cup soy flour
¼ cup wheat bran
1 teaspoon baking soda
½ teaspoon salt

Wet Ingredients

1½ cups buttermilk
¼ cup honey
2 tablespoons oil

This is a fine, simple dinner bread that is great served piping hot from the oven.

Mix together the dry ingredients.

Combine the wet ingredients.

Mix the dry and wet ingredients together. Pour into a well-greased medium-size loaf pan.

Bake at 325° F. for about 1 hour.

Let the bread cool for 10 minutes before removing it from the pan.

Wheat Germ Honey Bread

Dry Ingredients

1½ cups whole wheat flour
1 cup wheat germ
2 teaspoons baking powder
¼ teaspoon baking soda
¼ teaspoon salt

Wet Ingredients

¾ cup milk
¼ cup oil
¼ cup honey
1 egg, beaten

Proteins, iron, vitamin E, and B vitamins —that's what you get with this honey-flavored loaf. Using different kinds of honey changes the taste of this loaf considerably. For example, the strong taste of buckwheat honey makes this more like a molasses bread, while the mild taste of most supermarket brands merely adds the suggestion of a honey taste.

Mix together the dry ingredients.

Mix together the wet ingredients.

Combine the wet and dry ingredients lightly.

Pour the batter into a small greased loaf pan. Bake at 350° F. for 30 minutes.

Let the bread cool for 10 minutes before removing it from the pan.

Glenda's Protein Bread

Dry Ingredients

2 cups whole wheat flour
1½ cups unbleached flour
⅔ cup nonfat dry milk
⅓ cup wheat germ
2 teaspoons baking powder
½ teaspoon baking soda
½ teaspoon salt

Wet Ingredients

¾ cup orange juice
3 eggs
½ cup oil or softened butter
¼ cup light molasses
¼ cup honey
1 medium-size banana
½ cup raisins
⅓ cup chopped dried apricots
½ cup chopped dates

Glenda developed this to counter the image of dry, heavy, tasteless "health" breads. This is sweet, moist, fruity, and crunchy. It is especially high in protein.

Mix together the dry ingredients.

Combine the orange juice, eggs, oil or butter, molasses, honey, and banana in a blender. Blend until smooth. Add the raisins, apricots, and dates.

Combine the liquid-plus-fruit and dry ingredients lightly.

Spoon into a large greased loaf pan.

Bake at 325° F. for 60 to 70 minutes.

Let the bread cool for 10 minutes before removing it from the pan. This is a heavy bread and should be removed very gently.

Baked Boston Brown Bread

Dry Ingredients

2 cups whole wheat or graham flour
½ cup cornmeal
3 tablespoons soy flour
2 teaspoons baking soda
½ teaspoon salt
1 cup raisins

Wet Ingredients

¼ cup molasses
1 cup buttermilk

This is a somewhat unconventional Boston brown bread in that it is baked, not steamed.

Mix together the dry ingredients.

Mix together the wet ingredients.

Mix together the wet and dry ingredients.

Pour into a greased medium-size loaf pan. Let stand for 30 minutes.

Bake at 350° F. for 40 to 50 minutes.

Let the bread cool for 10 minutes before removing it from the pan.

Glenda's Coffee Oat Bread

Dry Ingredients

1½ cups oat flour
1½ cups unbleached flour
⅓ cup sugar
½ cup nonfat dry milk
¼ teaspoon salt
½ teaspoon cinnamon
1½ teaspoons baking powder

Wet Ingredients

2 tablespoons softened butter
1½ cups cold strong coffee
1 egg
1 teaspoon vanilla extract

This bread is not very sweet, and the coffee imparts a distinctive taste. For an even stronger coffee flavor, espresso can be substituted in full or in part for the coffee. Serve this bread with softened cream cheese.

Combine the dry ingredients in a mixing bowl.

Combine the butter, coffee, egg, and vanilla extract in a blender at a moderate speed until well blended.

Stir together the wet and dry ingredients. Spoon into a greased medium-size loaf pan.

Bake at 350° F. for 50 to 60 minutes.

Let the bread cool for 10 minutes before removing it from the pan.

Oatmeal Fruit Bread

Dry Ingredients

2 cups unbleached flour
1½ cups oat flour
¼ cup sugar
¼ teaspoon salt
2 teaspoons baking powder
½ teaspoon baking soda

Wet Ingredients

½ cup orange juice
½ cup pineapple juice
¼ cup orange marmalade (or pineapple preserves)
1 egg, beaten
1 tablespoon oil
1 cup chopped dried fruit

Use a combination of your favorite dried fruits for this bread—and don't forget the raisins. We like to include a little of everything: pears, peaches, nectarines, apricots, prunes, apples, and golden raisins. Cut the fruit into small pieces.

Mix together the dry ingredients.

Stir together the orange juice, pineapple juice, marmalade, egg, and oil. Add the dried fruit.

Combine the liquid-plus-fruit and dry ingredients.

Pour into a greased medium-size loaf pan.

Bake at 350° F. for 50 to 60 minutes.

Let the bread cool for 10 minutes before removing it from the pan.

Howard's Maple Oat Bread

Dry Ingredients

2 cups unbleached flour
1 cup oat flour
2 teaspoons baking powder
¼ cup maple sugar

Wet Ingredients

1½ cups milk
1 egg, beaten
1 tablespoon oil
¼ cup pure maple syrup
½ cup golden raisins

Howard has been experimenting with maple syrup and maple sugar for years. This was his first successful maple bread. It's a firm, chewy bread with the clear taste of maple. Be sure to use 100 percent maple syrup; pancake syrup just doesn't have enough maple taste to be used here.

Mix together the dry ingredients.

Mix together the milk, egg, oil, and maple syrup. Add the raisins.

Combine the wet and dry ingredients. Spoon into a greased medium-size loaf pan. Let it sit for 10 to 15 minutes before baking.

Bake at 350° F. for 35 to 40 minutes.

Let the bread cool for 10 minutes before removing it from the pan.

Heavy/Light Oat Bread

Dry Ingredients

1 cup whole wheat flour
1 cup oat flour
½ teaspoon salt
1 teaspoon baking soda
1 teaspoon cinnamon
½ cup dark raisins

Wet Ingredients

¼ cup honey
1 cup buttermilk
3 tablespoons melted shortening or oil
1½ teaspoons vanilla extract

When steamed, this bread has a very heavy texture and is better served after aging a day or so. Baked, this is a nice, light, whole grain bread that is excellent served warm.

Combine the dry ingredients.

Mix together the wet ingredients.

Pour the wet ingredients into the dry and combine just until moistened. Spoon the batter into a greased 7-cup mold (for a steamed bread) or a medium-size bread pan (for a baked bread).

To steam the bread, cover the mold with a double thickness of waxed paper or aluminum foil and tie it on securely. Place on a trivet or inverted heatproof bowl in a deep pot. Add enough boiling water to come halfway up the sides of the mold.

Cover the pot and steam for 1½ hours or until done.

To bake the bread, bake at 350° F. for about 1 hour.

Let the bread cool for 10 minutes before removing it from the pan.

Dill and Caraway Oat Bread

Dry Ingredients

1 cup oat flour
2 cups unbleached flour
½ cup nonfat dry milk
¼ teaspoon salt
2 teaspoons caraway seeds
1 teaspoon dill seeds
2 teaspoons baking powder

Wet Ingredients

1 cup water
1½ tablespoons oil
2 teaspoons malted barley syrup (brown
    sugar may be substituted)
1 egg, beaten

*This is a modest dinner bread with a pro-
nounced flavor of dill and caraway.*

Combine all the ingredients and spoon into
a greased medium-size loaf pan.

    Bake at 350° F. for 40 to 50 minutes.

    Let the bread cool for 10 minutes before
removing it from the pan.

Basic Rye Bread

Dry Ingredients

1 cup rye flour
1 cup unbleached flour
1 tablespoon sugar
¾ teaspoon baking soda
½ teaspoon baking powder
½ teaspoon salt
1 tablespoon caraway seeds

Wet Ingredients

6 tablespoons chilled butter
¾ cup milk
⅓ cup golden raisins (optional)

Mix together the dry ingredients.

Cut the butter into the dry ingredients with a pastry cutter or work it in with your fingers until it resembles coarse meal.

Mix in the milk and raisins.

Stir quickly, then spoon into a greased medium-size loaf pan. Bake at 375° F. for 45 minutes.

Let the bread cool for 10 minutes before removing it from the pan.

Dark Rye

Dry Ingredients

1½ cups rye flour
2½ cups unbleached flour
2 teaspoons baking powder
½ teaspoon salt
½ teaspoon baking soda
1 tablespoon caraway seeds
¼ teaspoon crushed fennel seeds

Wet Ingredients

1 cup buttermilk
½ cup milk
⅜ cup cold strong coffee
¼ cup oil
3 tablespoons light molasses
½ ounce unsweetened chocolate, melted
1 tablespoon cider or white vinegar

This is our quick bread version of a traditional old world black bread. The addition of vinegar gives it a light sourdough taste.

Combine the dry and wet ingredients. This makes a thick, heavy batter. Spoon it into a large greased loaf pan and let it sit for 15 to 20 minutes.

Bake at 350° F. for 45 to 50 minutes.

Let the bread cool for 10 minutes before removing it from the pan.

Potato Rye Bread

Dry Ingredients

1¾ cups rye flour
¾ cup unbleached flour
3 tablespoons nonfat dry milk
1 teaspoon baking powder
1 tablespoon caraway seeds
½ teaspoon salt

Wet Ingredients

½ cup drained cooked shredded potato
½ cup potato cooking water (reserve the rest to be used in soup or keep in the refrigerator for other breads)
2 tablespoons oil
2 tablespoons malted barley syrup or light molasses
1 tablespoon grated orange peel

Add potatoes to bread and you get a moister and lighter bread. To prepare the potato for the bread, peel and shred 1 small potato. Cook it in 1½ to 2 cups water (enough to cover the potato shreds fully) for about 10 minutes.

Combine all the ingredients. The batter will be very heavy. Place in a small greased loaf pan and let it sit for 15 to 20 minutes.

Bake at 350° F. for 45 minutes.

Let the bread cool for 10 minutes before removing it from the pan.

Triticale Bread

Dry Ingredients

2½ cups triticale flour
½ teaspoon cinnamon
¼ teaspoon salt
1 teaspoon baking soda

Wet Ingredients

1 egg, beaten
¼ cup molasses (or malted barley syrup)
¼ cup oil
Grated rind from 1 lemon
⅔ cup yogurt or sour cream

Triticale (pronounced trit-i-kay-lee) is a newly popular grain that is a cross between wheat and rye. It is very nutritious and, because the taste is mild, it is often liked by people who ordinarily don't like whole wheat. The cinnamon in this bread is very subtle and will be a nice mystery ingredient to most tasters.

Mix together the dry ingredients.

Combine the wet ingredients.

Mix together the wet and dry ingredients. The batter will be quite heavy. Spoon into a greased medium-size loaf pan.

Bake at 375° F. for about 45 minutes.

Let the bread cool for 10 minutes before removing it from the pan.

Basic Bran Bread

Dry Ingredients

2 cups wheat bran
1 cup unbleached flour
1½ teaspoons baking powder
¾ teaspoon baking soda
½ teaspoon salt

Wet Ingredients

1¼ cups buttermilk
1 egg, beaten
¼ cup honey

Combine all the ingredients. Pour into a small greased loaf pan.

Bake at 375° F. for 1 hour.

Let the bread cool for 10 minutes before removing it from the pan.

Bran Fig Bread

Dry Ingredients

1½ cups wheat bran
1½ cups unbleached flour
1½ teaspoons baking powder
¼ teaspoon salt

Wet Ingredients

1½ cups milk
½ cup dark brown sugar
¼ cup oil
¾ cup chopped figs

Figs and bran go together like rye and caraway seeds. While bran is strong tasting, it does not overwhelm the figs, especially if you use dried black mission figs.

Mix together the dry ingredients.

Combine the wet ingredients.

Combine the dry and wet ingredients. Spoon into a greased medium-size loaf pan.

Bake at 375° F. for 60 to 70 minutes.

Let the bread cool for 10 minutes before removing it from the pan.

Raisin Bran Bread

Wet Ingredients

1 cup raisins (dark or golden or
   a combination)
1½ cups warm water
1 egg, beaten
2 tablespoons oil
½ teaspoon vanilla extract

Dry Ingredients

1 cup wheat bran
1¾ cups unbleached flour
¾ cup light brown sugar
2 teaspoons baking powder
½ teaspoon baking soda

*This heavy, sweet brown bread is comple-
mented by mounds of cream cheese.*

To plump the raisins, combine the raisins
and water. Let stand for 30 minutes. Add
the egg, oil, and vanilla.

Combine the dry ingredients.

Combine the wet and dry ingredients
lightly. Spoon the batter into a well-
buttered 1-pound coffee can or several
smaller cans. (The cans should be about
two-thirds full.)

Bake at 350° F. for 50 to 60 minutes.

Let the bread cool for 10 minutes before
removing it from the can. Allow the flavors
blend overnight before serving. This bread
keeps well.

Date Bran Bread

Wet Ingredients

1 cup chopped dates
1 cup boiling water
1 egg
¼ cup honey
½ teaspoon vanilla extract

Dry Ingredients

¾ cup whole wheat flour
¾ cup unbleached flour
1 cup wheat bran
⅓ cup wheat germ
1 teaspoon baking powder
½ teaspoon baking soda
½ teaspoon salt
½ cup chopped nuts (optional)

This is an excellent fruit bread with a coarse texture. It is best served cold.

Combine the dates and boiling water. Set aside to cool.

Beat together the egg, honey, and vanilla. Add to the cooled date mixture.

Combine the dry ingredients.

Combine the wet and dry ingredients lightly. Spoon into a small greased loaf pan.

Bake at 350° F. for 1 hour.

Let the bread cool for 10 minutes before removing it from the pan.

TBS Light Buckwheat Bread

Dry Ingredients

1 cup light buckwheat flour
1½ cups unbleached flour
¼ cup sugar
1½ teaspoons baking powder
1 teaspoon baking soda
¼ teaspoon salt

Wet Ingredients

1 cup milk
1 egg, beaten
2 tablespoons oil

TBS was the acronym of The Baltimore School where we taught and experimented with bread baking for 5 oven-filled years. Howard developed this bread for all of those who love buckwheat pancakes. Even if you don't normally care for buckwheat, you will find this a wholesomely tasty bread.

Mix together the dry ingredients.

Mix together the wet ingredients.

Pour the wet ingredients into the dry and mix together lightly. Spoon into a greased medium-size loaf pan.

Bake at 350° F. for 40 to 45 minutes.

Let the bread cool for 10 minutes before removing it from the pan.

Jeanne's Rice Bread

Dry Ingredients

2¾ cups cream of rice (one 16-ounce package)

3 tablespoons sugar

¼ teaspoon salt

2 teaspoons baking powder

Wet Ingredients

1 cup milk

1 egg, beaten

3 tablespoons oil

This bread was inspired by one of our devoted tasters. The texture of this bread is like corn bread—except for the crunchy crust. If you bake this bread in mini-loaf pans or small cans, you increase the surface area and thus the crunchiness from the unusual rice crust.

Combine the dry ingredients.

Mix together the wet ingredients.

Combine the dry and wet ingredients. Pour into small greased cans (holding 1 to 1½ cups) or a small greased loaf pan. Fill close to the top since this bread will not rise very much.

Bake at 350° F. for about 45 minutes. Reduce the time by 5 to 10 minutes for the small pans.

Let the bread cool for 10 minutes before removing it from the pan.

Note

For variety and moistness, add 1½ medium-size bananas (mashed) and reduce the milk to ½ cup.

Buckwheat Groats Bread

Wet Ingredients

¼ cup buckwheat groats
½ cup water
6 tablespoons butter
¾ cup milk
2 tablespoons dark brown sugar

Dry Ingredients

1¾ cups unbleached flour
1 teaspoon baking soda
½ teaspoon baking powder

Now if you really want the full taste of buckwheat, this bread is it. It is very strong tasting, so we just make a small loaf.

First, prepare the groats. Combine the groats and water in the top of a double boiler and cook for about 30 minutes, or until all the water is absorbed (or follow the directions on the package).

While the groats are still warm, add the butter. Stir until the butter is melted and absorbed. Then add the milk and sugar.

Mix together the dry ingredients.

Combine the groats mixture with the dry ingredients.

Spoon the batter into a small greased loaf pan. Bake at 375° F. for 40 to 45 minutes.

Let the bread cool for 10 minutes before removing it from the pan.

3

Nut Flour, Seed, and Peanut Butter Breads

There is a doubly distinctive character to nut flours and seeds in breads. The flavor of the nut or seed used suffuses the bread, and the textures are different. These breads are generally rougher in texture and more crumbly than white flour or whole grain breads. They are not sandwich breads, but they can all be served with a main dish.

The seeds we use are mainly sunflower, sesame, and poppy. Usually you see these seeds as decorations. Here we actually bake them in the bread. They add an unusual crunchiness. Poppy seeds and sesame seeds are small enough so you don't have to crush or grind them. But peanuts, almonds, and sunflower seeds must be ground into a meal or "flour." It's really very easy. Just put the nuts into a blender or food processor and process until you have a coarse meal.

There are three things you should know about baking with nuts and seeds. The first is that the volume of whole nuts is different from the volume you get after grinding, and, for example, one cup of almonds will grind to a smaller volume than will one cup of sunflower seeds. What that means is that you measure after grinding. So one half cup of peanut flour means one half cup of peanut flour — and not one half cup of peanuts measured then ground.

Second, you should not buy commercially ground meals or grind large quantities yourself unless you plan to use it within a few days. Ground nuts and seeds can dry out or their natural oils turn rancid very quickly.

Finally, you can assure freshness by buying your nuts and seeds unroasted (and unsalted). You can roast them when you're ready. Put them on an ungreased baking sheet and bake at 350° F. until they begin to turn. Nuts can go from a light toast to an inedible dark brown in minutes so we begin checking constantly after the first 10 minutes.

Let the nuts or seeds cool before you grind them.

Peanut Rye Bread

Dry Ingredients

1 cup roasted unsalted peanuts
1 cup rye flour
3 tablespoons light brown sugar
1½ teaspoons grated orange peel
½ teaspoon salt
2 teaspoons baking powder

Wet Ingredients

¾ cup milk
3 tablespoons oil
⅓ cup golden raisins

This bread yields a good peanutty taste—not of peanut butter, but of peanuts. It has a very rough texture and a good, chewy quality.

First, grind the peanut "flour." Start with 1 cup roasted, unsalted peanuts and grind them in a blender or food processor until you have a coarse meal. Measure out ¾ cup peanut flour. Combine with the remaining dry ingredients.

Mix together the wet ingredients.

Combine the dry and wet ingredients and mix just until blended.

Place in a small greased loaf pan. Bake at 350° F. for 40 to 45 minutes.

Let the bread cool for 10 to 15 minutes before removing it from the pan.

Poppy Seed Bread

Dry Ingredients

2 cups unbleached flour
¼ cup brown rice flour
2 teaspoons baking powder
¼ teaspoon salt
¾ cup poppy seeds

Wet Ingredients

½ cup softened butter
½ cup sugar
1 egg
1 teaspoon vanilla extract
Grated rind of ½ lemon
1¼ cups milk

This bread is crust to crust seeds with just enough dough to hold them together. If you really love the taste and crunch of poppy seeds, use the ¾ cup of seeds called for in this recipe. If you are fainthearted, use only about ½ cup seeds.

Combine the dry ingredients.

Cream together the butter and sugar. Add the egg, vanilla, lemon rind, and milk. Mix well.

Mix together the wet and dry ingredients until just blended. Spoon into a small well-greased baking pan, roughly 6 by 12 inches.

Bake at 350° F. for 45 to 50 minutes.

Serve warm, directly from the pan. The bread will be about 1 inch high. Serve it in thin slices.

Whole Grain Poppy Seed Bread

Dry Ingredients

1¾ cups whole wheat flour
¼ cup brown rice flour
½ cup poppy seeds
½ teaspoon baking soda
1½ teaspoons baking powder
½ teaspoon salt

Wet Ingredients

¼ cup softened butter
1 egg, beaten
1 cup yogurt
3 tablespoons honey
1 teaspoon vanilla extract

Glenda developed this poppy seed dinner bread. It is an even-grained, nutritious, and tasty bread with plenty of poppy seed crunch. Experiment with the amount of seeds you add until it suits your taste. Serve it warm for dinner.

Do buy poppy seeds in bulk as they are outrageously expensive if purchased in grocery store tins.

Combine the dry ingredients.

Mix together the wet ingredients.

Mix together the wet and dry ingredients. Pour into a small greased loaf pan.

Bake at 350° F. for about 50 minutes.

Let the bread cool for 5 to 10 minutes before removing it from the pan.

White Poppy Seed Bread

Dry Ingredients

2 cups unbleached flour
½ cup brown rice flour
1 teaspoon baking powder
2 teaspoons baking soda
¼ teaspoon salt
⅓ cup white poppy seeds
½ cup sugar

Wet Ingredients

½ cup oil
¾ cup milk
1 egg, beaten
1 teaspoon vanilla extract

White poppy seeds are hard to find though they are used often in Indian and Middle Eastern confections. They are worth the hunt. White poppy seeds make an unusual bread. This recipe produces one small loaf of a somewhat crumbly, good-keeping, subtly nutty-tasting bread. Serve it any time.

Mix together the dry ingredients.

Combine the wet ingredients.

Combine the dry and wet ingredients. Pour into a small greased loaf pan.

Bake at 350° F. for about 45 minutes.

Let the bread cool in the pan for 10 minutes. Be gentle in removing it from the pan since it is fragile.

Sesame Seed Bread

Dry Ingredients

2 cups whole wheat flour or 2½ cups
   unbleached flour
⅓ cup sugar
2 teaspoons baking powder
½ cup sesame seeds
½ teaspoon salt

Wet Ingredients

¼ cup oil
2 eggs, beaten
⅔ cup milk

Sesame seeds are native to India and are rich in vitamins, minerals, and protein. They are especially rich in calcium and lecithin. This bread is permeated by the wonderful nutty taste of sesame; it makes another good dinner bread.

Combine the dry ingredients.

Beat together the wet ingredients.

Combine the wet and dry ingredients. Spoon the batter into a small greased loaf pan.

Bake at 350° F. for 40 to 50 minutes. Let the bread cool for 5 to 10 minutes before removing it from the pan. Serve warm or cold.

Sesame-Millet Bread

Dry Ingredients

1 cup millet flour
1 cup whole wheat flour
¼ cup brown rice flour
½ cup roasted sesame seeds
2 teaspoons baking powder
½ teaspoon salt
¼ teaspoon baking soda

Wet Ingredients

3 tablespoons honey
1 egg
¼ cup oil
1 cup yogurt

Sesame-millet is a very popular yeast bread in San Francisco. Glenda decided to experiment with making a quick bread after finding millet flour in a health food store. (Once again, you could make your own flour by pulverizing the seeds in a blender or food processor.) Millet is the seed of a type of grass plant. This is another bread that is best eaten warm.

Mix together the dry ingredients.

Beat together the wet ingredients.

Combine the wet and dry ingredients lightly. Spoon into a small greased loaf pan.

Bake at 350° F. for about 50 minutes.

Let the bread cool for 5 to 10 minutes before removing it from the pan.

Sunflower Rye Bread

Dry Ingredients

¾ cup sunflower meal
1 cup rye flour
¼ cup unbleached flour
2 teaspoons baking powder
3 tablespoons brown sugar
½ teaspoon cinnamon
½ teaspoon crushed anise
¼ teaspoon salt

Wet Ingredients

1 cup milk
3 tablespoons oil

We had never baked with sunflower seeds until we encountered Stella Standard's Our Daily Bread. *We adapted this recipe from her interesting collection. It has a rich, crunchy taste and rough texture.*

You can buy shelled sunflower seeds or sunflower meal in many health food stores; however, the meal usually comes in large cans. To ensure that the flavor and nutrition is at its best, grind your own.

Mix together the dry ingredients.

Mix together the wet ingredients.

Combine the dry and wet ingredients, mixing lightly. Spoon into a small greased loaf pan.

Bake at 350° F. for 35 minutes.

Let the bread cool for 10 minutes before removing it from the pan.

Carol's Peanut Butter Bread

Dry Ingredients

1¼ cups unbleached flour
¾ cup oat flour
2 tablespoons sugar
1 grated orange rind
½ teaspoon salt
2 teaspoons baking powder

Wet Ingredients

¼ cup smooth peanut butter
¼ cup oil
¾ cup milk

The taste is surprisingly rich and buttery, especially considering the small amount of peanut butter used. The bread crumbles and does not keep well; but fresh out of the oven, it makes even the most exacting peanut butter lover happy. We developed this recipe to satisfy our dear friend, Carol, who loves peanut butter baked goods and, needless to say, we enjoyed the challenge of satisfying her. This is a great bread for brunch or snacks.

Mix together the dry ingredients.

Mix together the wet ingredients.

Combine the wet and dry ingredients lightly. Spoon into a small greased loaf pan.

Bake at 375° F. for 50 minutes.

Let the bread cool for 10 minutes before removing it from the pan. This is a very fragile bread and requires gentle treatment. It slices best with a sharp bread knife.

Old-Time Peanut Butter Bread

Dry Ingredients

2 cups unbleached flour
⅓ cup sugar
½ teaspoon salt
2 teaspoons baking powder

Wet Ingredients

1 cup peanut butter
1¼ cups milk
2 eggs

Old-time peanut butter, or the kind you grind yourself at the food co-op, is known for the way it sticks to the roof of your mouth. This bread comes close to that old-fashioned quality.

Mix together the dry ingredients. Mix in the peanut butter.

Beat together the milk and eggs.

Combine the wet and dry ingredients lightly. Spoon into a small greased loaf pan.

Bake at 350° F. for 50 to 60 minutes.

Let the bread cool for 10 minutes before removing it from the pan.

4
Chocolate and Carob Breads

If you like chocolate and have never had a chocolate bread, you are certainly in for a surprise. If you don't feel strongly about chocolate, some of these breads may still appeal to you.

Those breads that call for unsweetened chocolate and ½ cup or less of sugar are dinner breads. They are just slighty sweeter than the typical dinner bread, and you can serve a chocolate bread just about any time.

The sweeter chocolate breads contain about 1 cup of sugar, and you will want to reserve these for breakfast, dessert, or snack time.

Feel free to vary the amount of sugar to your taste.

Chocolate Spice Bread

Dry Ingredients

2 cups unbleached flour
¼ cup sugar
½ teaspoon ginger
¼ teaspoon mace
¼ teaspoon nutmeg
¼ teaspoon cloves
¼ teaspoon cinnamon
1½ teaspoons baking soda

Wet Ingredients

¾ cup buttermilk
¼ cup light molasses
2 ounces unsweetened chocolate, melted

This highly spiced bread is dark, dense, and delightfully bitter. Serve it after it has cooled, so that the spices have a chance to blend and mellow. This can be a surprising accompaniment to curried dishes.

Combine the dry ingredients.
   Mix together the wet ingredients.
   Combine the wet and dry ingredients.
Pour into a small greased loaf pan.
   Bake at 325° F. for 30 minutes.
   Let the bread cool for 10 minutes before removing it from the pan.

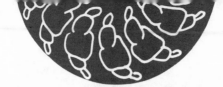

Sour Cream Chocolate Bread

Dry Ingredients

2¼ cups unbleached flour
1 teaspoon baking powder
½ teaspoon baking soda
½ teaspoon salt

Wet Ingredients

½ cup sugar
2 eggs
1 cup sour cream
6 tablespoons grated semi-sweet chocolate

Swirling the chocolate throughout produces a marbled appearance. This is a dessert bread that also goes well at breakfast with eggs. For dessert, it is an unusual accompaniment for fruit.

Combine the dry ingredients.

Beat together the sugar, eggs, and sour cream.

Combine the wet and dry ingredients. Add the grated chocolate.

Spoon the batter into a small greased loaf pan allowing the grated chocolate to swirl about. Be careful, if you stir too hard, you will lose the marbling effect.

Bake at 350° F. for 40 to 50 minutes.

Let the bread cool for 10 minutes before removing it from the pan.

Cherry Chocolate Bread

Dry Ingredients

3 cups unbleached flour
1 tablespoon baking powder
1 cup white sugar
½ teaspoon salt
6 ounces semi-sweet chocolate bits

Wet Ingredients

3 ounces unsweetened chocolate, melted
1 cup milk
¼ cup oil
¼ cup undyed maraschino cherry juice
½ cup drained, chopped maraschino
   cherries
1 egg, beaten

This bread breaks the cake barrier. It is a dessert bread that is as close to a cake as icing. Label this "for chocolate lovers everywhere."

Combine the dry ingredients.
   Combine the wet ingredients.
   Combine the wet and dry ingredients.
Spoon into a large greased loaf pan.
   Bake at 350° F. for 60 to 70 minutes.
   Let the bread cool for 10 minutes before removing it from the pan.

Potato Chocolate Bread

Wet Ingredients

1 medium-size potato
Water
¾ cup milk
2 eggs, beaten
½ cup oil
1 ounce melted or grated unsweetened
   chocolate
½ teaspoon vanilla extract

Dry Ingredients

2½ cups unbleached flour
½ cup sugar
½ teaspoon salt
½ teaspoon baking powder
½ teaspoon baking soda

This is an elegant bread. The potato gives it a moistness and texture that is surprising. It has a definite chocolate taste, but it is not a sweet bread. Set it off against a sharp cheese, such as cheddar or Wensleydale, and you have an exciting contrast.

First prepare the potato. Shred the potato, cover generously with water, and cook for 5 minutes. Drain the potato.
Your yield should be about 1 cup.

Mix together the remaining wet ingredients. Add the potato.

Combine the dry ingredients.

Mix together the dry and wet ingredients. Pour into a greased medium-sized loaf pan.

Bake at 350° F. for 50 to 60 minutes.

Let the bread cool for 10 minutes before removing it from the pan.

Variation

Chocolate Zucchini Bread. Normally we don't change a single ingredient in a recipe and claim it is a new recipe. But the Potato Chocolate Bread becomes a very different bread just by changing one ingredient.

The zucchini acts the same way as the potato; it brings and retains moisture in the loaf. You will not taste the zucchini, but you will clearly see its green flecks, and the bread will be a delightful conversation piece.

Follow the Potato Chocolate Bread recipe, but substitute 1 cup of shredded (not grated) zucchini for the potato. Do not cook the zucchini.

Double Carob Bread

Dry Ingredients

1 cup light rye flour
1 cup whole wheat flour
¼ cup carob powder
½ cup carob chips
1 teaspoon baking powder
½ teaspoon salt

Wet Ingredients

2 tablespoons softened butter
⅓ cup honey
1 egg, beaten
1 cup milk

Carob isn't chocolate; chocolate lovers can't be fooled that easily. It is, however, a taste even chocolate lovers can appreciate, and it is richer in vitamins and minerals, lower in fat (about 1/10 the amount), with half the calories of chocolate. This bread is hearty and not too sweet. It is best served cold.

Combine the dry ingredients.

Combine the wet ingredients in a blender and mix well.

Pour the wet ingredients into the dry and stir together lightly. Spoon into a small greased loaf pan.

Bake at 350° F. for about 50 minutes.

Let the bread cool for 10 minutes before removing it from the pan.

5
Fruit Breads

The most exciting feature of quick breads is their ability to incorporate fruits and fruit blends. We spent seven years experimenting with fruits, and these recipes are the outcome of a lot of baking and tasting —and fun.

Whether the recipe calls for fresh or dried fruit, you should always use the best-tasting you can find. Don't use badly bruised or aging "fresh" fruit, and don't use rock-hard dried fruit.

When to serve fruit breads is a matter of personal taste. Some are clearly dessert or snack breads; they usually have half a cup or more of sugar. They will all go well at a brunch or as a late evening snack. Some of the breads, because of their contrasting flavors, can be served with selected main dishes.

Basic Apple Bread

Dry Ingredients

2½ cups unbleached flour
½ cup sugar
2 teaspoons baking powder
½ teaspoon baking soda
½ teaspoon salt

Wet Ingredients

2 large tart apples, peeled and grated
2 eggs
¼ cup softened butter
¼ cup apple juice or cider
2 tablespoons lemon juice

The challenge of baking with apple is that of preserving the apple flavor through the baking process. Applesauce and apple butter seem to work better than raw apples as a rule, but this basic apple bread will give you a hint of apple.

Mix together the dry ingredients.

Combine the wet ingredients in a blender. Process until smooth.

Combine the wet and dry ingredients lightly. The batter will be very heavy. Spoon into a greased medium-size loaf pan.

Bake at 325° F. for about 70 minutes.

Let the bread cool for 10 minutes before removing it from the pan.

Apple Butter Bread

Dry Ingredients

1½ cups unbleached flour
½ cup oat flour
½ teaspoon salt
2 teaspoons baking powder

Wet Ingredients

2 eggs
1 cup apple butter
¼ cup apple juice or cider
½ cup chopped nuts (optional)
½ cup raisins (optional)

While plain apples hint of themselves in bread, apple butter will hit you over the palate. Apple butter is produced by cooking apples until they are very thick. Cinnamon and cloves are typically added, imparting both taste and the rich brown coloring. Most commercial apple butters are heavily sweetened and so there is no need for additional sweeteners to be added to the bread.

Combine the dry ingredients.

Beat together the eggs, apple butter, and apple juice. Add the nuts and raisins.

Mix the dry and wet ingredients. Spoon the batter into a small greased loaf pan.

Bake at 350° F. for 55 minutes.

Let the bread cool for 10 minutes before removing it from the pan.

Apple Cheddar Bread

Dry Ingredients

2 cups unbleached flour
¼ cup sugar
½ teaspoon salt
1½ teaspoons baking powder
½ teaspoon baking soda
½ cup grated cheddar cheese

Wet Ingredients

¼ cup softened butter
2 eggs, beaten
Juice from 1 lemon
3 apples, peeled and grated (about 1 cup)

A sharp cheddar is a fine complement to a tart apple. Glenda's father used to say, "Apple pie without cheese is like a kiss without a squeeze." In this bread we combine the two to produce a moist loaf that preserves this taste combination. It makes a good dinner bread.

Combine the dry ingredients.

Mix together the wet ingredients.

Stir the wet and dry ingredients together until just moistened. Pour into a greased medium-size loaf pan.

Bake at 350° F. for about 1 hour.

Let the bread cool for 10 minutes before removing it from the pan.

Spiced Applesauce Bread

Dry Ingredients

1¾ cups unbleached flour
¾ teaspoon baking soda
½ teaspoon baking powder
¼ teaspoon salt
½ teaspoon cinnamon
¼ teaspoon allspice
Grated rind of 1 lemon

Wet Ingredients

½ cup chilled butter
2 eggs, yolks separated
1 cup applesauce
½ cup chopped pecans (optional)
⅓ cup raisins (optional)

This is much like an applesauce cake, but better. Serve warm with butter, or cold with cream cheese. It is also a nice addition to a cheese plate. Or an empty plate.

Combine the dry ingredients. Cut the butter into the flour mixture.

Mix together the egg yolks and applesauce. Combine with the dry ingredients. Add the pecans and raisins, if desired.

Whip the egg whites until stiff.

Gently fold the egg whites into the batter. Pour the batter into a greased medium-size loaf pan.

Bake at 350° F. for about 45 minutes, or until golden brown.

Let the bread cool for 10 minutes before removing from the pan.

Apple Oat Bread

Dry Ingredients

1¼ cups unbleached flour
¾ cups oat flour
½ teaspoon baking powder
¼ teaspoon baking soda
½ teaspoon salt
1 teaspoon cinnamon
¼ teaspoon nutmeg
½ cup raisins
½ cup chopped dates

Wet Ingredients

½ cup softened butter
½ cup brown sugar
1 cup grated tart apple
½–¾ cup buttermilk

This may be one of the slowest quick breads we've made, but it is worth the wait. The preparation is routine, but we bake this in a slow, steamy oven. With these spices and fruits and the moist, slow baking, you have a bread that is quite close to a fruitcake.

Mix together the dry ingredients.

Cream together the butter and sugar. Add the apple and buttermilk.

Combine the wet and dry ingredients. Spoon into a greased medium-size loaf pan.

Bake at 275° F. for about 2 hours. Put a large pan of hot water in the oven to create steam while the bread is baking.

Let the bread cool for 10 minutes before removing it from the pan.

Howard's Apricot Bread

Wet Ingredients

⅔ cup chopped dried apricots
Water
1 egg
1 cup milk
3 tablespoons oil
4 teaspoons grated orange rind

Dry Ingredients

2 cups unbleached flour
2 teaspoons baking powder
½ cup sugar
½ teaspoon salt

Keep in mind three things when baking with dried apricots. First, use California dried apricots that still have their characteristic color. Second, cut the apricots into small pieces. Third, let the cut apricots sit in warmed orange juice or water for at least 30 minutes before adding to a batter.

Put the apricots in a saucepan. Cover with water. Simmer for 15 minutes. Drain and cool. Beat together the egg, milk, oil, and orange rind. Add the cooled apricots.

Combine the dry ingredients.

Combine the wet and dry ingredients and stir just until mixed. Pour into a greased medium-size loaf pan.

Bake at 375° F. for about 1 hour.

Let the bread cool for 10 minutes before removing it from the pan.

Apricot Almond Bread

Wet Ingredients

½ cup orange juice
⅔ cup chopped dried apricots
½ cup milk
1 egg, beaten
3 tablespoons oil

Dry Ingredients

1½ cups unbleached flour
¼ cup brown rice flour
¼ cup almond meal or almond powder
½ cup sugar
½ teaspoon salt
2 teaspoons baking powder

Combine the orange juice and apricots in a saucepan. Heat gently; then let it sit for 15 to 30 minutes.

Combine the milk, egg, and oil. Add the apricots and orange juice.

Combine the dry ingredients.

Combine the wet and dry ingredients. Pour into a greased medium-size loaf pan.

Bake at 375° F. for 50 to 60 minutes.

Let the bread cool for 10 minutes before removing from the pan.

Note

Almond powder is available at many Chinese groceries. Or you can make your own almond meal by pulverizing blanched almonds in a blender or food processor.

Apricot Orange Bread

Wet Ingredients

⅔ cup chopped dried apricots
1 cup orange juice
1 egg
2 tablespoons oil

Dry Ingredients

2 cups unbleached flour
1 cup whole wheat flour
¼ cup white sugar
¼ cup brown sugar
2 teaspoons baking powder
¼ teaspoon baking soda
½ teaspoon salt

This is a whole grain bread, contrasting the nuttiness of whole wheat with the tartness of the apricots and orange.

Combine the apricots and orange juice in a saucepan and heat gently. Let cool for about 30 minutes.

Beat together the egg and oil. Add the cooled apricots and orange juice.

Combine the dry ingredients.

Combine the wet and dry ingredients. Turn into a large greased loaf pan.

Bake at 350° F. for about 1 hour.

Let the bread cool for 10 minutes before removing from the pan.

Banana Oat Flake Bread

Wet Ingredients

1 cup sliced banana
⅓ cup molasses
Juice and grated rind of 1 orange
1 egg
⅓ cup oil

Dry Ingredients

2 cups oat flake cereal
2 cups unbleached flour
2 teaspoons baking powder
¼ teaspoon salt

Banana bread is one of the best-known quick breads. Who hasn't tasted several versions of this black-flecked sweet bread? Because the banana makes the bread moist, it keeps well. This bread is best served warm.

Combine the wet ingredients in a blender or food processor. Blend well. Stir the oat flakes into the wet ingredients and allow to soak while you prepare the remaining dry ingredients.

Combine the flour, baking powder, and salt.

Mix together all the ingredients. Pour into a greased medium-size loaf pan.

Bake at 350° F. for 60 minutes.

Let the bread cool for 10 minutes before removing it from the pan.

Whole Wheat Banana Bread

Dry Ingredients

¾ cup unbleached flour
¾ cup whole wheat flour
1 teaspoon baking soda
½ teaspoon salt

Wet Ingredients

½ cup softened butter
½ cup sugar
1 egg, beaten
¼ cup buttermilk (or yogurt or sour cream)
2 medium-size bananas, mashed

This is another not-too-sweet or over-powering banana bread.

Combine the dry ingredients.

Cream together the butter and sugar. Add the egg, buttermilk, and banana. Mix well.

Combine the wet and dry ingredients. Mix just enough to combine well. Pour into a small greased loaf pan.

Bake at 350° F. for 50 to 60 minutes.

Let the bread cool for 10 minutes before removing it from the pan.

Banana Apricot Bread

Dry Ingredients

2 cups unbleached flour
½ cup chopped almonds
⅓ cup sugar
¼ teaspoon salt
1½ teaspoons baking powder
½ teaspoon baking soda
¾ cup finely chopped dried apricots

Wet Ingredients

3 small bananas, sliced
2 eggs
⅓ cup softened butter

Even people who don't like banana bread found this an unusual treat. The apricot adds a nice tartness.

Combine the dry ingredients.

Mix the wet ingredients in a blender or food processor. Blend until smooth.

Combine the wet and dry ingredients. Spoon into a greased medium-size loaf pan.

Bake at 350° F. for about 1 hour.

Let the bread cool for 10 minutes before removing it from the pan.

Banana Nut Bread

Dry Ingredients

2 cups unbleached flour
½ teaspoon salt
½ teaspoon baking soda
½ cup chopped walnuts

Wet Ingredients

½ cup softened butter
½ cup brown sugar
2 eggs
1 cup sliced bananas

This makes a very crunchy bread. It keeps well if refrigerated.

Combine the dry ingredients.

Combine the wet ingredients in a blender. Mix until smooth.

Combine the dry and wet ingredients. Pour into a greased medium-size loaf pan.

Bake at 350° F. for about 45 minutes.

Let the bread cool for 10 minutes before removing it from the pan.

Orange Honey Bread

Dry Ingredients

2½ cups unbleached flour
2 teaspoons baking powder
½ teaspoon baking soda
½ teaspoon salt
¾ cup chopped hazelnuts or pecans

Wet Ingredients

2 tablespoons softened butter
¾ cup honey
1 egg, beaten
¾ cup orange juice
1½ tablespoons grated orange rind

This is one of those quick breads that sits on the border between a cake and a bread. Sweet and rich in orange flavor, it also surprises the taste with the addition of nuts.

Mix together the dry ingredients.
　Combine the wet ingredients.
　Stir the wet ingredients into the dry. Pour into a greased medium-size loaf pan.
　Bake at 325° F. for about 1 hour.
　Let the bread cool for 10 minutes before removing it from the pan.

Three Orange Bread

Dry Ingredients

2 cups unbleached flour
1 cup oat flour
½ cup sugar
2 teaspoons baking powder
1 teaspoon baking soda
½ teaspoon salt

Wet Ingredients

¾ cup orange juice
¼ cup orange marmalade
1 teaspoon grated orange rind
1 egg, beaten
¼ teaspoon vanilla extract

There are many ways to get a good orange flavor in an orange bread. Grated orange rind is the simplest and the best way. You can buy grated orange peel, or you can grate it fresh yourself; or you can dry and pulverize the peels for future use. Peel the orange before juicing or eating; dry the peel (free of the white membrane) in a sunny window. The dried peel will be hard. You can pulverize it in a food processor or (clean) coffee mill. Orange juice, as well as undiluted concentrate, is good for flavoring, as is orange marmalade.

In this bread we pulled out all stops and used juice, rind, and marmalade. The result is that the orange flavor and color permeates the bread. It has a good, firm texture, and it is not too sweet to serve with a meal.

Combine the dry ingredients.

Mix together the wet ingredients.

Mix together the dry and wet ingredients. Spoon into a well-greased medium-size loaf pan.

Bake at 350° F. for 50 minutes.

Let the bread cool for 10 minutes before removing it from the pan.

Orange Potato Bread

Wet Ingredients

1 small potato
Water
¾ cup orange juice
¼ cup marmalade
¼ cup oil
1 egg, beaten

Dry Ingredients

3 cups unbleached flour
½ cup sugar
2 teaspoons baking powder
1 teaspoon baking soda
¼ teaspoon salt

With the potato in this bread, you have a moist, orange, semi-sweet loaf.

First, shred the potato. Cook it in water to cover for about 10 minutes. Drain. Measure out ½ cup cooked shredded potato. Add the remaining wet ingredients to the potato. Mix well.

Combine the dry ingredients.

Mix together the wet and dry ingredients. Spoon into a well-greased medium-size loaf pan.

Bake at 350° F. for 50 minutes.

Let the bread cool for 10 minutes before removing it from the pan.

TBS Pear Bread

Dry Ingredients

3 cups unbleached flour
⅓ cup nonfat dry milk
¼ cup sugar
½ teaspoon salt
1 tablespoon baking powder
4 dried pear halves, diced

Wet Ingredients

1½ cups pear nectar
1 egg
3 tablespoons oil

In our search for new challenges, we decided to see if we could develop some tasty pear breads. Since pears have such a mild flavor, this was not an easy task. When we served this to our students, they found it exciting. Few had even conceived of a pear bread. The contrast of the deep brown crust with the white interior and almost translucent fruit made this a visually, as well as viscerally, stimulating experience. Serve this any time with softened butter.

Combine the dry ingredients.

Beat together the wet ingredients.

Mix together the wet and dry ingredients. Spoon into a large greased loaf pan.

Bake at 350° F. for about 1 hour.

Let the bread cool for 10 minutes before removing it from the pan.

Triple Pear Bread

Dry Ingredients

2½ cups unbleached flour
4 dried pear halves, finely diced
¼ cup sugar
½ teaspoon salt
2 teaspoons baking powder
½ teaspoon ground ginger or 1-inch
  piece of fresh ginger root, grated

Wet Ingredients

1 pear, peeled, cored, and sliced
¼ cup pear nectar
1 egg
1 tablespoon oil

Combine the dry ingredients.

Combine the wet ingredients in a blender or food processor.

Blend until smooth.

Combine the wet and dry ingredients very lightly. Pour into a well-greased medium-size loaf pan.

Bake at 350° F. for about 1 hour. If the bread still seems as though it isn't done, turn off the oven and let it continue baking as the oven cools. This seems to be the only effective way to deal with fruit breads that don't want to get done.

Let the bread cool for 10 minutes before removing it from the pan.

Pear, Date, and Bran Bread

Dry Ingredients

2 cups unbleached flour
½ cup wheat bran
¼ cup sugar
¼ teaspoon salt
2 teaspoons baking powder
¼–½ cup chopped dates

Wet Ingredients

½ cup milk
1 egg, beaten
2 tablespoons oil
2 pears, peeled and shredded
  (about 1 cup)
Grated rind of 1 lemon

Bartlett pears have such an unobtrusive taste that their flavor is almost lost in a bread with a strong flour such as bran. Pear apples, which are abundant in Chinese markets in August, or seckel pears give this bread its unique flavor.

Combine the dry ingredients.

Mix together the wet ingredients.

Mix together the dry and wet ingredients. Spoon into a small greased loaf pan. Let the bread sit for 20 minutes.

Bake at 350° F. for about 1 hour. When the bread is golden brown, turn off the oven and leave it in the oven to finish cooking the inside.

Let the bread cool for 10 minutes before removing it from the pan. This is excellent served cold.

Coconut Pineapple Bread

Dry Ingredients

3 cups unbleached flour
2 slices unsweetened dried pineapple, chopped
½ teaspoon salt
1 tablespoon baking powder
1 teaspoon grated orange rind

Wet Ingredients

1¼ cups coconut pineapple juice
1 egg, beaten
3 tablespoons oil

Would any cookbook be complete without the popular piña colada taste? This is not a sweet bread and has an excellent texture. Introduced at one of our school meetings, it was a big hit with its light, subtle taste. Eat it plain. It goes well with coffee.

Combine the dry ingredients.

Mix together the wet ingredients.

Mix the dry and wet ingredients together lightly. Spoon into a large greased loaf pan.

Bake at 350° F. for about 45 minutes.

Let the bread cool for 10 minutes before removing it from the pan.

Pineapple Cheese Bread

Dry Ingredients

2½ cups unbleached flour
2 teaspoons baking powder
½ teaspoon baking soda
¼ teaspoon salt
1 tablespoon sugar
¾ cup shredded muenster cheese

Wet Ingredients

1 cup pineapple juice
1 egg, beaten
2 tablespoons oil
½ cup chopped dried unsweetened
   pineapple

This is an unusual combination. The cheese makes the bread rich and smooth. Dried pineapple, which you can buy at health food stores if your grocery store doesn't stock it, gives this bread its distinctive taste. Toasting the bread renews the cheese flavor. Served with butter, Pineapple Cheese Bread goes with almost everything.

Combine the dry ingredients.

Mix together the juice, egg, and oil. Add the pineapple.

Combine the wet and dry ingredients. Spoon the batter into a greased medium-size loaf pan.

Bake at 350° F. for 45 minutes.

Let the bread cool for 10 minutes before removing it from the pan.

Pineapple Prune Bread

Dry Ingredients

2½ cups unbleached flour
2 teaspoons baking powder
½ teaspoon salt
½ cup chopped prunes
½ cup chopped dried unsweetened
   pineapple

Wet Ingredients

3 tablespoons honey
¼ cup milk
1 cup pineapple juice
1 egg
3 tablespoons oil

This is a rich, moist bread that is good combined with cheese or served as a breakfast or snack bread.

Mix together the dry ingredients.

Beat together the wet ingredients.

Combine the wet and dry ingredients. Spoon into a well-greased medium-size loaf pan.

Bake at 350° F. for 60 to 70 minutes.

Let the bread cool for 10 minutes before removing it from the pan. This is best served after it ages for a few hours.

Basic Prune Bread

Dry Ingredients

1 cup unbleached flour
1 cup whole wheat pastry flour
1 teaspoon baking soda
1 teaspoon baking powder
¼ teaspoon salt

Wet Ingredients

1 cup buttermilk
¼ cup malted barley syrup
2 tablespoons oil
½ cup finely diced prunes

Not everyone likes prunes, but even "prun-ophobes" can relish a prune bread. In the following two recipes, we vary the flours. As you will see, the breads take on a differ-ent taste as the prune interacts with the flours.

Combine the dry ingredients.

Mix together the buttermilk, barley syrup, and oil. Add the prunes.

Combine the wet and dry ingredients. Mix gently. Spoon into a small greased loaf pan.

Bake at 350° F. for 50 to 60 minutes.

Let the bread cool for 10 minutes before removing it from the pan.

Light Prune Bread

Dry Ingredients

1¼ cups unbleached flour
½ cup oat flour
¼ cup brown rice flour
1 teaspoon baking powder
¼ teaspoon salt

Wet Ingredients

1 cup buttermilk
¼ cup malted barley syrup
2 tablespoons oil
½ cup finely diced prunes

In this variation of the basic prune bread we replaced the whole wheat flour with oat flour and brown rice flour. The result? A sweet nuttiness and a fine-textured, crunchy crust. This bread is outstandingly golden brown in color from the combination of ingredients.

Combine the dry ingredients.

Mix together the buttermilk, barley syrup, and oil. Add the prunes.

Combine the wet and dry ingredients. Mix gently and spoon into a small greased loaf pan.

Bake at 350° F. for 50 to 60 minutes.

Let the bread cool for 10 minutes before removing it from the pan.

Prune Pecan Bread

Dry Ingredients

1½ cups unbleached flour
1½ cups oat flour
½ cup light brown sugar
2 teaspoons baking powder
¼ teaspoon mace
¼ teaspoon nutmeg
¼ teaspoon salt

Wet Ingredients

1⅓ cups milk
1 egg, beaten
¼ cup oil
½ cup chopped prunes
½ cup chopped pecans

This is a sweet, crumbly, crunchy, nutty, spiced loaf. It is distinctive in taste and texture.

Combine the dry ingredients.

Mix together the milk, egg, and oil. Add the prunes and pecans.

Combine the wet and dry ingredients. Spoon into a large greased loaf pan.

Bake at 350° F. for 50 to 60 minutes.

Let the bread cool for 10 minutes before removing it from the pan.

Cherry Bread

Dry Ingredients

2 cups unbleached flour
1 teaspoon baking soda
½ teaspoon salt

Wet Ingredients

½ cup softened butter
½ cup sugar
1 cup buttermilk
1 teaspoon vanilla extract
2 eggs, beaten
1 cup chopped pitted cherries
1 cup chopped pecans

This is a rich bread that can serve as dessert, perhaps accompanied by a mild cheese. It is good warm or cold.

Combine the dry ingredients.

Cream together the butter and sugar. Add the buttermilk, vanilla, eggs, cherries, and pecans.

Combine the wet and dry ingredients lightly. Spoon into a greased medium-size loaf pan.

Bake at 350° F. for 55 to 60 minutes.

Let the bread cool for 10 minutes before removing it from the pan.

Cranberry Bread

Dry Ingredients

2 cups unbleached flour
½ cup sugar
1 tablespoon grated orange rind
½ teaspoon salt
1½ teaspoons baking powder
½ teaspoon baking soda

Wet Ingredients

¾ cup orange juice
¼ cup oil
1 cup coarsely chopped cranberries

This is a striking bread. Not only do the bright red cranberries stand out, but their tartness embedded in this somewhat sweet dough adds still another contrast. You can prolong the cranberry season by freezing berries and defrosting them just before baking this bread.

Combine the dry ingredients.

Mix together the wet ingredients.

Mix the dry and wet ingredients lightly. This makes a thick batter. Spoon into a small greased loaf pan.

Bake at 350° F. for 50 to 60 minutes.

Let the bread cool for 10 minutes before removing it from the pan.

Purple Plum Bread

Dry Ingredients

3 cups unbleached flour
¼ cup sugar
2 teaspoons baking powder
½ teaspoon salt
1⅓ cups chopped canned plums, drained well

Wet Ingredients

1 egg
¾ cup milk
½ cup orange juice
1 tablespoon grated orange rind
3 tablespoons oil

This was one of the first quick breads we ever made. The moistness of the plums calls for a longer baking time, but the bread still remains quite soft. It ages well and freezes well. Serve it with softened cream cheese for a good taste contrast.

Combine the dry ingredients.

Beat together the wet ingredients.

Combine the wet and dry ingredients. Pour into a large greased loaf pan. Allow to stand for about 20 minutes.

Bake in a preheated 350° F. oven for approximately 70 minutes.

Let the bread cool for 10 minutes before removing it from the pan.

Raspberry Bread

Dry Ingredients

3 cups unbleached flour
½ teaspoon salt
¾ teaspoon cream of tartar
½ teaspoon baking soda

Wet Ingredients

½ cup softened butter
½ cup sugar
1 teaspoon rum or rum flavoring
1 tablespoon lemon juice
4 eggs
1 cup raspberry preserves
½ cup sour cream

This is a rich, decadent bread. The high fat and sugar content makes this dessert bread something you might want to serve at tea time or after a light meal.

Combine the dry ingredients.

Cream together the butter, sugar, rum or rum flavoring, and lemon juice. Beat in the eggs.

Stir together the raspberry preserves and sour cream.

Add the sour cream mixture alternately with the flour mixture to the sugar-egg mixture. Mix lightly. Spoon into a large greased loaf pan.

Bake at 350° F. for 50 to 60 minutes.

Let the bread cool for 10 minutes before removing it from the pan.

Blueberry Orange Bread

Dry Ingredients

3 cups unbleached flour
2 teaspoons baking powder
¼ teaspoon baking soda
½ teaspoon salt
1 cup fresh, frozen, or drained canned
   berries

Wet Ingredients

¼ cup honey
Grated rind and juice of 1 orange
½ cup milk
½ cup oil

This was one of our very popular breads—good served hot, but even better the next day. Serve it to people who love blueberry muffins. Black raspberries make an unusual substitute for blueberries.

Combine the dry ingredients and stir to blend thoroughly.

Beat together the wet ingredients.

Pour the wet ingredients into the dry and stir until the dry ingredients are moist. Spoon into a large well-greased loaf pan and let it stand for about 15 minutes.

Bake in a 350° F. oven for 1 hour.

Let the bread cool for 10 minutes before removing it from the pan.

6
Vegetable Breads

In fruit breads, the flavor of the fruit remains distinct. In vegetable breads, usually only the most sensitive of palates are able to identify the vegetable. Mainly vegetables add color, moistness, and texture to a bread batter.

Corn breads are the unique American addition to vegetable bread making. Native Americans introduced corn and cornmeal to the newcomers who proceeded to bake an extraordinary variety of stove-top and oven-made breads.

The most common cornmeal varieties are yellow and white. Few people can distinguish their taste in baked goods, though we do prefer the yellow for its warm, rich color. There is a natural sweetness and graininess to corn bread that, along with its color, makes it unmistakable.

Blue cornmeal is rare and somewhat expensive. It is grown on less than 1 percent of all the acres of edible corn, and it is harder to grow and harvest. But it's just as easy to cook with. You will find it somewhat sweeter and less grainy than its paler counterparts. When you add wet ingredients, the bluish-purple meal makes a bluish gray batter.

While you can substitute the blue cornmeal in any recipe, we have a strong preference for it in the Sour Cream Corn Bread (page 108).

Carrot Orange Bread

Dry Ingredients

2 cups unbleached flour
1 teaspoon baking soda
½ teaspoon salt
½ cup raisins

Wet Ingredients

3 medium-size carrots, chopped
⅔ cup milk
½ cup softened butter
3 tablespoons honey
2 eggs

Glaze Ingredients

⅓ cup honey
⅓ cup undiluted orange juice concentrate

This is a very rich, moist bread that is great for a picnic lunch. It can even serve as dessert after a light meal.

Mix together the dry ingredients.

Combine the wet ingredients in a blender or food processor. Process until smooth.

Combine the dry and wet ingredients. Pour into a greased 9-inch round pan.

Bake at 350° F. for about 1 hour.

Let the bread cool for 10 minutes before removing it from the pan.

To make the glaze, combine the honey and orange juice concentrate and pour over the top of the bread.

The bread may be served immediately. Leftover bread should be stored in the refrigerator.

Sweet Carrot Bread

Dry Ingredients

2¼ cups unbleached flour
¾ cup whole wheat flour
2 teaspoons baking powder
½ cup candied fruit or white raisins
½ teaspoon salt
1 teaspoon cinnamon
¼ teaspoon nutmeg

Wet Ingredients

1 egg
½ cup molasses
¼ cup oil
1½ cups grated carrots
¾ cup buttermilk

Mix together the dry ingredients.

Combine the wet ingredients in a blender and process until smooth.

Mix together the wet and dry ingredients just until blended. Spoon into a large greased loaf pan.

Bake at 375° F. for about 1 hour.

Let the bread cool for 10 minutes before removing it from the pan.

New England Corn Bread

Dry Ingredients

1 cup cornmeal
1 cup unbleached flour
2 teaspoons cream of tartar
1 teaspoon baking soda
½ teaspoon salt

Wet Ingredients

1 cup milk
1 egg
¼ cup melted butter
¼ cup pure maple syrup

While corn breads have been associated with Southern cookery, this variation, which relies on maple syrup, has no regional bounds.

Mix together the dry ingredients.

Combine the wet ingredients in a blender and process until smooth.

Combine the dry and wet ingredients, mixing gently but well. Spoon into a flat buttered 8-inch or 9-inch square baking pan.

Bake at 400° F. for 25 to 30 minutes.

Serve warm, directly from the pan. Or let cool for 5 to 10 minutes, then remove from the pan.

Southwestern Corn Bread

Dry Ingredients

1¼ cups cornmeal
½ cup unbleached flour
½ teaspoon salt
2 teaspoons baking powder
¼ cup nonfat dry milk

Wet Ingredients

2 eggs, beaten
¾ cup water
¼ cup oil
3 or 4 chopped jalapeño peppers
1 cup shredded sharp cheddar cheese
½ medium-size onion, grated

Add some jalapeño peppers, cheese, and onion and you produce another regional variation. This is a genuinely zesty bread. It makes a tasty accompaniment to soup.

Mix together the dry ingredients.

Combine the eggs, water, and oil. Beat well. Add to the dry ingredients. Then mix in jalapeños, cheese, and onion. Pour into a lightly greased 8-inch or 9-inch baking pan.

Bake at 425° F. for about 30 minutes.

Serve warm directly from the baking pan. Or let it cool for 10 minutes, then remove it from the pan.

Coconut Corn Bread

Dry Ingredients

1 cup unbleached flour
¾ cup cornmeal
1 tablespoon baking powder
½ teaspoon salt

Wet Ingredients

1 cup coconut milk
¼ cup oil
1 egg, beaten
⅓ cup shredded sweetened coconut (if you use unsweetened coconut, add 3 tablespoons sugar)

You can add a substantial number of ingredients to a basic corn bread. As long as you adjust the wet ingredients so your batter isn't too runny, you can pretty much count on a successful outcome. In this basic recipe, we substituted coconut milk for plain milk and then added shredded coconut to enhance the flavor and texture. This is a good time to extend the "white theme" by using white cornmeal.

Mix together the dry ingredients.

Mix together the wet ingredients.

Combine the dry and wet ingredients. Spoon into a buttered 8-inch or 9-inch baking pan.

Bake at 400° F. for 25 to 30 minutes.

Let the bread cool for 10 minutes before removing it from the pan.

Sour Cream Corn Bread

Dry Ingredients

1 cup cornmeal
¾ cup unbleached flour
3 tablespoons sugar
1½ teaspoons cream of tartar
1 teaspoon baking soda
½ teaspoon salt

Wet Ingredients

1 cup sour cream
¼ cup milk
1 egg
2 tablespoons oil

We don't know who first substituted sour cream for milk or water, but it was a brilliant stroke in the art of baking. The sour cream changes the texture of the bread. The graininess is almost gone, but the thick crumb of corn bread remains — as does its sweetness.

Mix together the dry ingredients.

Beat together the wet ingredients.

Combine the dry and wet ingredients. Spoon into a well-buttered 8-inch or 9-inch baking pan.

Bake for 10 minutes at 375° F.; then reduce the heat to 350 F. and bake for 15 minutes more.

Serve warm, directly from the baking pan. Or let it cool for 10 minutes, then remove it from the pan.

7
Special Dessert and Holiday Breads

Kugelhupf Bread

Wet Ingredients

¼ cup softened butter

⅓ cup honey (or malted barley)

2 eggs, beaten

1 cup milk

1 teaspoon grated lemon rind

½ teaspoon vanilla extract

Dry Ingredients

2½ cups whole wheat pastry flour

1 cup golden raisins

2 teaspoons baking powder

¼ teaspoon nutmeg

½ teaspoon cinnamon

½ teaspoon salt

3 ounces sliced almonds

This is an unusual version of a traditional holiday favorite. In its traditional form, it is made with yeast and white flour and baked in a fluted tube pan. This whole wheat adaptation will amaze you with its lightness of texture and taste.

Beat together the wet ingredients.

Combine the dry ingredients, except the almonds.

Mix together the wet and dry ingredients.

Pour some of the sliced almonds into the bottom of a greased medium-size bread pan. Pour the batter into the pan. Sprinkle the remaining sliced almonds over the top.

Bake in a 350° F. oven for about 1 hour.

Let the bread cool for 10 minutes before removing it from the pan.

Christmas Bread

Dry Ingredients

3 cups unbleached flour
2 teaspoons baking powder
¾ teaspoon salt
⅓ cup raisins

Wet Ingredients

¼ cup honey
3 eggs
½ cup sliced banana
½ cup orange juice
½ teaspoon vanilla extract
1½ cups chopped mixed dried fruits

This is a delicious bread to serve any time, but it is especially festive for the holidays. Many find this a welcome relief from the overly sweet holiday treats. The citrus flavor enchances any combination of dried fruits that you choose—apricots, prunes, pineapple, raisins, pears, peaches.

Mix together the dry ingredients.

Combine the honey, eggs, banana, orange juice, and vanilla in a blender. Process until smooth. Add to the dried fruits.

Combine the wet and dry ingredients, mixing well. Spoon into a large greased loaf pan.

Bake at 350° F. for about 1 hour.

Let the bread cool for 10 minutes before removing it from the pan.

Stollen

The Fruits

⅓ cup golden raisins
⅓ cup chopped citron
⅓ cup currants
¼ cup chopped candied orange peel
¼ cup candied lemon peel
¼ cup chopped candied pineapple
¼–½ cup cognac

Wet Ingredients

1 cup milk
1 egg, beaten
2 tablespoons oil
1½ teaspoons grated lemon peel
¼ teaspoon vanilla extract

Dry Ingredients

3 cups unbleached flour
1 tablespoon baking powder
¼ cup sugar

Stollen is one of the best-known traditional Christmas breads. There may be as many varieties as there are bakers.

Combine all the fruits in a mixing bowl. Add the cognac and let the fruits soak for 1 to 2 hours.

Beat together the wet ingredients. Drain the fruits, discarding the remaining cognac, then add to the wet ingredients.

Combine the dry ingredients.

Mix together all the ingredients. This is a heavy batter, almost like a yeast bread. Place in a large greased loaf pan. Or, if you

want the traditional stollen shape, knead it briefly on a lightly floured board. Shape it into an oval, about 10 inches long. With the flat edge of a knife, crease it off center lengthwise. Using your hand, roll one side of the crease so it overlaps the other.

Bake at 375° F. for 40 minutes.

Let the bread cool for 10 minutes before removing it from the pan.

Sweet Potato Cranberry Bread

Dry Ingredients

2½ cups unbleached flour
½ teaspoon salt
1½ teaspoons baking powder
½ teaspoon baking soda
½ teaspoon cinnamon
¼ teaspoon nutmeg
⅛ teaspoon mace

Wet Ingredients

¾ cup cold baked sweet potato, sliced
½ cup milk
2 eggs
¼ cup softened butter
⅓ cup molasses
1 cup raw cranberries

This festive holiday bread tastes of tart cranberries and spices. It keeps well for several days; some like it better when the flavors have had a chance to blend and the cranberries are not so tart.

Combine the dry ingredients.

Combine the wet ingredients in a blender or food processor and process until the cranberries are coarsely chopped.

Combine the wet and dry ingredients. Pour into a large well-greased loaf pan.

Bake at 350° F. for about 1 hour.

Let the bread cool for 10 minutes before removing it from the pan.

Mincemeat Bread

Dry Ingredients

2½ cups unbleached flour
2 teaspoons baking soda

Wet Ingredients

1 (28-ounce) jar mincemeat
1⅓ cups sweetened condensed milk
2 eggs, beaten
1 ounce rum

Mix together the dry ingredients.

Combine the wet ingredients.

Mix together the dry and wet ingredients. Spoon into a greased medium-size loaf pan.

Bake at 300° F. for 1½ to 2 hours. Check the bread for firmness at the end of the first 90 minutes. Remove it from the oven when it has a firm feel and a good hollow sound.

Let the bread cool for 10 minutes before removing it from the pan.

Gingerbread

Dry Ingredients

2¼ cups unbleached flour
2 tablespoons finely chopped crystallized ginger
1 teaspoon cinnamon
1 teaspoon baking soda

Wet Ingredients

1 cup dark beer, at room temperature
½ cup oil
½ cup light molasses
1 egg, beaten

This is the most unusual gingerbread recipe we've tried. We found it in an article on beer. It works. The dark beer adds to and complements the ginger. Do use a good dark beer.

Combine the dry ingredients.

Mix together the wet ingredients.

Combine all ingredients, mixing well. Spoon into a greased 9-inch square baking pan.

Bake at 325° F. for 45 to 50 minutes.

Let the bread cool for 10 minutes before removing it from the pan.

8
Scones and Muffins

It is hard to describe a scone to someone who has never eaten one. It's lighter than a biscuit, smoother than an English muffin, heavier than a muffin, and thicker than a flat bread. Of course, you'll have to try it.

Scones come in different sizes and shapes; some are oven-baked, some cooked on a griddle or frying pan, and some are griddle-cooked and then oven-finished. They originated in Scotland, Wales, and parts of Northern England. Their variations in size—the large ones have been called bannocks in Scotland—and in ingredients seems to reflect the different regions in which they developed.

Our scones are surely modern American variations, and our basic griddle scone is made with one of Howard's favorite ingredients, sour cream.

While scones are fairly new to American kitchens, everybody knows and likes muffins. The possible variations are amazing, and you can even bake several types at the same time.

There are a few ground rules for muffin making. First, mix your batter very gently. Second, expect muffin batters to be lumpy. Third, grease your muffin cups well—including the top of the pan. Fourth, fill your muffin cups about two-thirds to no more than three-quarters full. Note that all our muffin recipes are designed to fill the standard twelve-cup muffin pan. Finally, after they are baked, usually at high temperatures, let the muffins stay in the pans for about five minutes after they come out of the oven. This way you can be able to remove them easily and keep them in one piece.

Remember that muffins don't keep; they are best eaten right after baking. But if you do have some left over, reheat with moist heat. You can, for example, put the leftover muffins in a small paper bag, sprinkle in about a teaspoon of water, close the bag and heat at 450° F. for five to eight minutes.

Griddle Scones

Dry Ingredients

2 cups unbleached flour
2 teaspoons sugar
1 teaspoon baking soda
1 teaspoon cream of tartar
¼ teaspoon salt

Wet Ingredients

¾ cup sour cream

Combine the flour, sugar, baking soda, cream of tartar, and salt. Add the sour cream and mix briskly.

Place the dough on a floured board. Divide the dough in half and pat out each half to form a circle about ½ inch thick. The circle should be 5 to 6 inches in diameter.

Dust an ungreased griddle or frying pan with flour, add a scone, and cook over low heat. The scone will rise slightly. It will brown in 7 to 10 minutes, depending on the pan. When it is lightly browned, turn it over to brown the other side. Repeat with the second scone. Cut into quarters and serve warm.

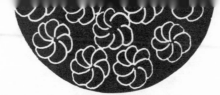

Modern Scotch Scone

Dry Ingredients

1½ cups unbleached flour
½ cup oat flour
1 teaspoon baking soda
2 tablespoons sugar
¼ teaspoon salt

Wet Ingredients

⅓ cup butter
⅔ cup milk
¼ cup currants (or ⅓ cup dark raisins)

In this recipe we use "modern" flours and add currants for a taste bonus. This is a fairly sweet bread.

Mix together the dry ingredients.

Cut the butter into the dry ingredients with a pastry cutter or work it in with your fingers until the mixture resembles cornmeal. Add the milk and currants.

Knead on a lightly floured board for about 3 minutes. Shape into an 8-inch circle. Place in a lightly greased frying pan.

Bake at 375° F. for 20 to 25 minutes.

Serve warm, directly from the pan.

Whole Wheat Scones

Dry Ingredients

1 cup whole wheat flour
1 cup unbleached flour
½ teaspoon baking soda
½ teaspoon cream of tartar
¼ teaspoon salt

Wet Ingredients

¾ cup buttermilk
2 tablespoons oil

Scones have been adapted to the growing interest in whole grains. Here's one tasty variation.

Combine the dry ingredients.

Mix together the wet ingredients.

Mix together all the ingredients and knead for about 3 minutes on a floured board. Divide the dough in half and pat each half into a 5-inch or 6-inch circle about ½ inch thick.

Lightly dust an ungreased griddle or frying pan with flour, add the scone, and cook over low heat for 7 to 10 minutes. When it has lightly browned, turn to brown the other side. Serve warm.

Orange Scone

Dry Ingredients

2½ cups unbleached flour
2 tablespoons sugar
1 teaspoon baking powder
1 teaspoon baking soda
½ teaspoon salt

Wet Ingredients

¾ cup orange juice
2 tablespoons oil
1 tablespoon grated orange rind
1 egg, beaten

Yellow-orange in color, moist, and thick-crumbed, this oven-baked American scone makes a good dinner bread. It is not sweet, but it is very orange in flavor. This recipe yields one large scone.

Mix together the dry ingredients.
Mix together the wet ingredients.
Combine the wet and dry ingredients.
Spoon into a greased 8-inch round pan.
Bake at 425° F. for 15 minutes.
Serve warm, directly from the pan.

Traditional Bannock

Dry Ingredients

1 cup instant oatmeal flakes
1 cup cornmeal
1 teaspoon baking soda

Wet Ingredients

1 cup buttermilk
2 tablespoons oil
2 tablespoons honey

In this traditional Scottish recipe, oatmeal and cornmeal are used. The bannock is first set in a greased frying pan and then finished in a medium-hot oven. The result is a hard-crusted and chewy scone.

Mix together the dry ingredients.

Mix together the wet ingredients.

Combine all the ingredients, mixing well. Spoon into a heated, greased frying pan.

Fry on low heat for about 5 minutes a side. Place the pan in a 375° F. oven and bake for 10 to 15 minutes.

Serve warm, directly from the pan.

The 1933 Muffin

Dry Ingredients

2 cups unbleached flour
2 tablespoons sugar
2 teaspoons baking powder
¼ teaspoon salt

Wet Ingredients

1 cup milk
1 egg, beaten
¼ cup oil

The best basic muffin we bake is one Howard found in a 1933 home baking book published by General Foods. The reason we call it a "basic" muffin is that you can add to it. In season, we might throw in some cranberries or blueberries. You can add mashed banana, cherries, cheddar cheese. Whatever you add, don't add more than a tablespoon to each muffin.

Combine the dry ingredients.

Mix together the wet ingredients.

Stir together the dry and wet ingredients, mixing gently. Spoon into a well-greased muffin pan.

Bake at 425° F. for 25 minutes.

Let the muffins cool for 5 minutes before removing them from the pan.

Note

If you are going to use a single filling for all the muffins, then simply add 1 cup of the filling to the batter. If you are using fruits, be sure they are well-drained. Cheese should be shredded. To add different fillings to a single batch, first spoon in the batter to fill one-third of the muffin cup. Next, add 1 heaping tablespoon of the filling. Then cover with enough batter to fill the muffin cup a bit over two-thirds full.

Bran Muffins

Dry Ingredients

1½ cups unbleached flour
1 cup bran
1 tablespoon grated orange rind
1 teaspoon baking soda
¼ teaspoon salt

Wet Ingredients

1 cup buttermilk
¼ cup light molasses
¼ cup oil

A popular, chewy, and firm muffin incorporates bran as a central ingredient. Bran muffins are everywhere in San Francisco. Glenda has sampled all of the "best," and recommends that you experiment with the theme by adding carrot, banana, raisin, prune, sesame seeds, nuts, or apple as your mood varies.

Combine the dry ingredients.
   Mix together the wet ingredients.
   Stir together the dry and wet ingredients.
Spoon into a well-greased muffin pan.
   Bake at 350° F. for 25 minutes.
   Let the muffins cool for 5 minutes before removing them from the pan.

Nutty Muffins

Dry Ingredients

1½ cups whole wheat pastry flour
¼ cup soy flour
1 tablespoon baking powder
¼ teaspoon salt
1¼ cups chopped roasted unsalted
   peanuts
⅓ cup roasted unsalted sunflower seeds
¼ cup roasted sesame seeds

Wet Ingredients

1 cup milk
¼ cup oil
¼ cup malted barley syrup (or honey)
1 egg, beaten
⅓ cup currants

This is one of those heavy, healthy, crunchy concoctions that will titillate your taste buds and have your diners calling for the chef.

Mix together the dry ingredients.

Mix together the wet ingredients.

Combine the dry and wet ingredients. Mix gently and spoon into a well-greased muffin pan.

Bake at 375° F. for 15 to 20 minutes.

Let the muffins cool for 5 minutes before removing them from the pan.

127

Old-Fashioned Oatmeal Muffins

Dry Ingredients

1⅔ cups unbleached flour
2 teaspoons brown sugar
2 teaspoons baking powder
¼ teaspoon salt

Wet Ingredients

1½ cups warm milk
1 cup cooked oatmeal
2 eggs
1 tablespoon softened butter

Brown sugar and oatmeal were probably the staples of those who began experimenting with our 1933 Muffin (see page 124). It's still good today, especially if you have any leftover cereal.

Combine the dry ingredients.
Beat together the wet ingredients.
Combine the wet and dry ingredients.
Spoon into a well-greased muffin pan.
Bake at 425° F. for 20 to 25 minutes.
Let the muffins cool for 5 minutes before removing them from the pan.

Oat Muffins

Dry Ingredients

1 cup oat flour
¾ cup unbleached flour
¼ cup brown rice flour
1 tablespoon baking powder
¼ cup sugar

Wet Ingredients

1 cup milk
3 tablespoons oil
1 egg, beaten

The sweet nuttiness of oat flour with a little brown rice flour added for the crust yields a delicious and different muffin.

Mix together the dry ingredients.
Mix together the wet ingredients.
Combine the dry and wet ingredients.
Spoon into a well-greased muffin pan.
Bake at 425° F. for 20 minutes.
Let the muffins cool for 5 minutes before removing them from the pan.

Beer and Cheese Muffins

Dry Ingredients

2 cups unbleached flour
2 tablespoons sugar
1 tablespoon baking powder
¼ teaspoon dry mustard

Wet Ingredients

1 cup beer, at room temperature
¼ cup oil
1 egg, beaten
1¼ cups (about 5 ounces) grated sharp
   cheddar cheese

What could go better with a glass of beer and a slice of cheese than a beer and cheese muffin? This tangy muffin is also appropriate for serving with soups or salads.

Combine the dry ingredients.

Combine the beer, oil, and egg. Mix well. Add the cheese.

Stir together all ingredients. Spoon into a well-greased muffin pan.

Bake at 400° F. for 20 to 25 minutes.

Let the muffins cool for 5 minutes before removing them from the pan.

9
Flat Breads and Crackers

Flat breads are genuinely quick breads. The batters tend to be thick, and they are patted down to about half an inch in height. Given their large surface area, they bake quickly. In fact, flat breads are probably the quickest of the quick breads. These recipes serve four, and are best when right out of the oven accompanied by plenty of sweet butter.

We included a section on crackers not because we believe that everyone should abandon the convenience of the store-bought ones but because many don't realize that crackers weren't always made by machines and delivered, double-wrapped, in a box. It is fun to experiment with making these crackers, especially if you can engage your friends or children in the experience. Don't expect them to taste exactly like your favorite brand—these are different. You may like them even more.

Finnish Barley Flat Bread

Dry Ingredients

2 cups barley flour
2 teaspoons sugar
2 teaspoons baking powder
¾ teaspoon salt

Wet Ingredients

1 cup light cream
2 tablespoons oil

This flat bread, known also as rieska, has a very grainy texture and the distinctive taste of barley flour. Although the ingredients are few and the preparation is simple, this is one of the great breads of the world. Serve it straight from the oven.

Combine the dry ingredients.

Combine the wet ingredients.

Combine the dry and wet ingredients, mixing quickly. Spoon onto a greased 15-inch baking sheet or a 12-inch pizza pan.

Pat the dough into a circle with an approximate diameter of 12 inches. The dough will not be more than ½ inch thick. Prick all over with a fork.

Bake at 450° F. for 10 minutes.

Cut into wedges. Serve warm, directly from the oven.

Quick Onion Flat Bread

Dry Ingredients

1⅓ cups unbleached flour
¼ teaspoon salt
2 teaspoons baking powder

Wet Ingredients

¼ cup plus 2 tablespoons water
2½ tablespoons oil

Topping Ingredients

2 tablespoons butter
¼ cup minced onion
1 egg, beaten
1 tablespoon water
1 teaspoon poppy seeds
1 teaspoon sesame seeds

Mix together the dry ingredients.

Mix together the wet ingredients.

Combine the wet and dry ingredients. Knead the bread gently on a lightly floured board for about 1 minute. Pat it out to a thickness of about ½ inch onto a greased 12-inch pizza pan.

Melt the butter in a frying pan over low heat. Add the onions and fry gently over low heat until golden.

Brush the top of the bread with a beaten egg to which you have added 1 tablespoon of water. Distribute the onions over the bread, then sprinkle with the poppy seeds and sesame seeds.

Bake at 500° F. for 8 to 10 minutes. Serve warm, directly from the oven.

Sunflower Barley Flat Bread

Dry Ingredients

1½ cups barley flour
¼ cup unbleached flour
¼ cup sunflower meal
1 tablespoon sugar
¾ teaspoon salt
1 tablespoon baking powder

Wet Ingredients

1 cup milk
2 tablespoons oil

Mix together the dry ingredients.

Combine the wet ingredients.

Stir together the wet and dry ingredients. Spoon the batter onto a well-greased 15-inch baking sheet. Pat the dough into a 12-inch circle about ½ inch thick. Prick all over with a fork.

Bake at 450° F. for 10 minutes. Serve warm, directly from the oven.

Note

Barley flour and sunflower seeds are both available in health food stores. To make sunflower meal, pulverize ½ cup of roasted unsalted sunflower seeds in a blender or food processor. Measure out the amount needed.

Chappatis

1½ cups whole wheat flour
½ cup water

Indian cookery has an extraordinary variety of quick flat breads. Often they are fried in clarified butter, though many are baked.

Mix together the flour and water. Knead in the mixing bowl for a few minutes. Cover with a damp towel and let it rest for about 20 minutes.

Form the dough into about 8 balls. Clap each ball in your hands until somewhat flattened. Place on a floured surface and flatten until a very thin 6-inch circle is formed.

Bake on heated, ungreased skillet for a few minutes. Turn when the surface begins to bubble. Brown the other side. They will be lightly puffed when done. Serve hot.

Coconut Chappatis

½ cup unbleached flour
⅓ cup unsweetened shredded coconut
¼ teaspoon salt
Pinch of white or cayenne pepper
3–5 tablespoons water

Mix the flour, coconut, salt, and pepper. Work in the water to make a firm dough.

Divide the dough into 6 parts. On a well-floured board, roll each piece into a small circle about 3 inches in diameter.

Cook the breads in a generously buttered frying pan until they are lightly browned on both sides.

To keep warm until ready to serve, cover with a towel and place them in a 250° F. oven.

Pooris

4 cups whole wheat flour
1 teaspoon salt
¼ cup ghee (clarified butter) or oil
2 cups yogurt

This is an Indian fried bread that is traditionally served with curries.

Combine all the ingredients. Knead the dough on a floured surface until it has a good spring to it. Cover the bowl and let stand at room temperature for about 30 minutes.

On a lightly floured surface, roll out the dough very thin. Cut into saucer-size pancakes about 6 inches in diameter. Fry in ½ inch of very hot clarified butter or oil until the poori is a light brown color. Drain on paper, and continue until all are cooked.

Pooris may be served hot or cold. To keep them warm while the full batch is fried, place them on paper towels in a baking dish in a 250° F. oven.

A Basic Cracker

Dry Ingredients

2 cups unbleached flour
½ teaspoon salt
½ teaspoon baking powder

Wet Ingredients

¼ cup chilled butter
½ cup milk
1 egg, beaten

Mix together the dry ingredients.

Cut the butter into the flour mixture until with a pastry cutter or work it in with your fingers until the mixture is mealy in appearance. Add the milk and egg.

Knead thoroughly on a lightly floured surface until the dough has a good spring to it. Then roll the dough out very thin. Cut into squares or rounds and place on greased baking sheets. Prick the crackers with a fork. Expect 4 to 5 dozen standard-size crackers.

Bake in 400° F. oven for 10 minutes.

Remove from the oven and using a spatula, place the crackers on wire racks to cool.

Rye Crackers

Dry Ingredients

1 cup rye flour
1 cup unbleached flour
½ teaspoon salt

Wet Ingredients

½ cup milk
½ cup melted butter

Combine the dry ingredients.

Mix together the wet ingredients.

Mix together all the ingredients and knead until the dough develops a light springiness. On a lightly floured board, roll the dough into ropes with a diameter of about 1 inch. Cut off thin slices and roll each slice so you have about a 3-inch cracker. You should get close to 4 dozen crackers. Place on lightly greased baking sheets.

Bake at 400° F. for 10 minutes or until lightly browned.

Remove the crackers from the sheets and cool on wire racks.

Graham Crackers

Dry Ingredients

2 cups whole wheat pastry or graham
    flour
½ teaspoon salt
1 teaspoon baking soda

Wet Ingredients

¼ cup honey
½ cup sour cream

This cracker was named after Dr. Graham, a mid-nineteenth century nutritionist who advocated eating whole wheat rather than white flour.

Combine the dry ingredients. Stir in the wet ingredients.

Knead gently in the mixing bowl for about 2 minutes. On a floured board, roll out the dough to about ¼ inch thick.

Cut into whatever cracker size you prefer, then gently transfer wtih a spatula to 15-inch greased baking sheets using a spatula.

Bake in a 375° F. oven for about 10 minutes.

Remove the crackers from the sheets and cool on wire racks.

Whole Wheat Oat Crackers

Dry Ingredients

1¾ cups whole wheat flour
1 tablespoon sesame seeds
1 cup quick-cooking oats
½ teaspoon baking soda

Wet Ingredients

¼ cup unsalted softened margarine
¾ cup buttermilk

Sometimes called a hardtack, this is a crisp, rough-textured cracker. This no-salt, reduced fat recipe comes from the Consumer Nutrition Institute.

Combine the dry ingredients, reserving ¼ cup of the oats.

Cream together the margarine and dry ingredients. Add the buttermilk. Mix lightly. Divide the dough in half, and flatten each half to form a square about 7 inches across. Refrigerate until the dough is firm. (You can speed up the process by placing the dough in the freezer for 20 to 30 minutes.)

When ready, roll out the dough on a well-floured surface. Each half should fill a

standard large baking sheet of 14 inches by 17 inches. Oil the baking sheets, then sprinkle with the remaining oats. Put the dough on the sheets and pat it out to fill the space. Prick the dough all over with a fork. Then cut into cracker sizes (a pastry wheel or pizza cutter will do a good job).

Bake at 325° F. for 15 to 20 minutes. The crackers should be golden brown and crisp.

Remove crackers to wire racks and allow them to cool thoroughly.

Potato Crackers

1 cup mashed potatoes
1½ cups unbleached flour (more if the
    potatoes are moist, less if they are dry)
½ cup butter, melted

Mix all the ingredients together to form a stiff dough ball. Divide the dough into fourths and roll out each portion on a well-floured board. Try to get the dough thinner than ⅛ of an inch. Gently place the dough on greased baking sheets.

Bake at 375° F. for 10 to 12 minutes. The crackers are done when they begin to brown. While still soft, cut into whatever-sized crackers you prefer and place on a cooling rack.

Index

NOTES

NOTES

NOTES

NOTES

NOTES

NOTES

NOTES

NOTES

NOTES